The Formula Book 2

The Formula Book 2

NORMAN STARK

SHEED ANDREWS AND McMEEL, INC.
Subsidiary of Universal Press Syndicate
KANSAS CITY

CAUTION TO READERS

In writing *The Formula Book 2*, I have excluded hazardous materials wherever possible, but in some cases they must be included to make a product effective. In making a formula, the reader should observe any note of caution added at the end of the recipe and consult Appendix D (Definitions of Chemicals) for cautions which may be specific to any ingredient.

We all know that materials such as waxes and oils will burn, so I have concentrated the warnings to materials that may be less familiar. But remember, *all* chemicals, including ordinary table salt, should be kept out of the reach of children, carefully labeled, and used only for the purpose they are intended.

The value and safety to you of the products in this book depend upon your careful use of the materials shown in the proportions given, as well as your observing any special cautions appearing in the book or with the materials. Neither I nor the publisher can be responsible for the efficacy of the products or your own safety if you do not follow these instructions and precautions.

First printing, August 1976   Second printing, September 1976

THE FORMULA BOOK 2 © 1976 by Stark Research Corporation. All rights reserved. Printed in the United States of America. No part of this book may be used or reproduced in any manner whatsoever without written permission except in the case of brief quotations embedded in critical articles and reviews. For information address Sheed Andrews and McMeel, Inc., a subsidiary of Universal Press Syndicate, 6700 Squibb Road, Mission, Kansas 66202.

Library of Congress Cataloging in Publication Data

Stark, Norman.
    The formula book 2.

    Companion to the author's Formula book, 1975.
    Includes index.
    SUMMARY: Non-technical instructions for turning basic chemical compounds into personal care, animal care, garden, and household products.
    1. Recipes. [1. Recipes] I. Title.
T49.S82   602   76-25975
ISBN 0-8362-0675-4
ISBN 0-8362-0676-2 pbk.

To my wife and partner Eileen

Contents

FOREWORD   11

INTRODUCTION: Why; Basic Equipment; Raw Materials and Where to Get Them; Some Helpful Hints   13

1. AROUND THE HOUSE
    Adhesive Tape Remover   23
    Alcohol-Resistant Treatment for Wood   23
    Antiseptic Cleaner — All Purpose   24
    Antistatic Spray for Rugs   27
    Baking Pan Antistick   27
    Bathtub and Sink Cleaner   28
    Blackboard Cleaner   31
    Carpet Cleaner   31
    Ceramic Tile Cleaner   32
    Christmas Tree Fire Retardant and Needle Preservative   32
    Coffee Extract   33
    Dance Floor Wax   34
    Fire Extinguishing Powder   37
    Fireplace Flame Colors   37
    Fireplace Flue Soot Remover   38
    Fire Retardant Paper   38
    General Purpose Deodorant and Disinfectant   39
    Grass Stain Remover   40
    Heating or Cooling Filter Cleaning Compound   40
    Ice Cube Release   41
    Library Paste   41
    Liquid Porcelain Cleaner   42
    Lubricating Stick   42
    Mildewproofing for Book Bindings   43
    Moth Repellent   44
    Oil and Grease Spot Remover   45

Paint and Wall Cleaner	46
Range Cleaner and Polish	46
Refrigerator Deodorant	47
Sink Disposal Cleaner	48
Soapless Rug Cleaner	48
Vinyl Cleaner	51
Wallpaper Remover	51
Water Softener — All Purpose	52
Wood Floor Bleach II	53

2. PERSONAL

Antiperspirant Foot Powder	59
Astringent Skin Cream	59
Baby Oil II	60
Baby Powder	63
Ballpoint Ink Remover for Hands	63
Bay Rum	64
Beauty Clay	64
Blackhead Remover	65
Callus Softener	66
Cuticle Remover	66
Dandruff Treatment	67
Disinfectant for Shoes	68
Dry Hand Cleaner	68
Earwax Softener	69
Effervescent Bath Salts	70
Eyelash and Eyebrow Conditioner	71
Face Lotion	72
Face Powder	72
Facial Bleach	73
Facial Pore Closer	74
Finger Stain Remover	74
Foot Powder	75
Lanolin Hand and Face Lotion	76
Leather Cleaner	76
Liquid Underarm Deodorant	77
Oxygen Foot Bath	78
Protective Hand Cream	78
Rubbing Alcohol Compound	79
Tar and Nicotine Stain Remover for Hands	79

Toilette Water	80
Underarm Deodorant Pads	81
Winter Hand Protective Lotion	81

3. AUTOMOTIVE AND MECHANICAL

Auto Fuel Ice Preventative	87
Automobile and Boat Top Dressing	87
Auto Windshield Cleaner	88
Auto Windshield Insect Remover	88
Gasoline Vapor Lock Compound	89

4. GARDEN AND AGRICULTURAL

Acidifying or Alkalizing Potted Plant Soil	93
Ant Repellent	93
Caterpillar Tree Bands	94
Chemical Flower Garden	95
Compost Making	95
Garden Insecticide — All Purpose	97
Hydroponic Plant Food	98
Potted Plant Fertilizer	99
Rabbit Repellent II	100

5. FOR SPORTS AND CAMPING

Barbecue Flame Extinguisher	105
Boot Dubbing	105
Canvas Fire Retardant	106
Fishline Dressing	109
Golf Ball Distance Improver	109
Mosquito Repellent	110
Shotgun and Rifle Cleaning and Polishing Cloth	111
Waterproofing Matches	112

6. ANIMAL CARE

Animal Bath Powder	117
Animal Dandruff Treatment	117
Animal Deodorant Spray	118
Animal Earache Oil	121
Animal Eczema Treatment	121
Animal Eyewash	122

Cat Litter Box Deodorant 125
Dog and Cat Coat Dressing 125
Flea Spray 126
Mange Treatment 126

7. SAFETY AND FIRST AID 133
Carbon Tetrachloride 136
Chlorine/Ammonia 137

APPENDICES
Appendix A: The Four Categories of Formulas
  Found in *The Formula Book 2* 139
Appendix B: Conversion Equivalents 141
Appendix C: Temperature Conversion Tables 147
Appendix D: Definitions of Chemicals Used
  in *The Formula Book 2* 149
Appendix E: A Treatise on Denatured Alcohols 159
Appendix F: Selection of Materials 169
Appendix G: Utensils and Equipment 171
Appendix H: Formulating Procedures 177
Appendix I: Sources of Chemicals 179
Appendix J: pH Preferences of Some Plants 185

INDEX 191

Foreword

The Formula Book 2 is the second volume of the series that will become a complete set over the coming years. *The Formula Book 1* was published in November 1975 and became an immediate success, reaching the best-seller list.

Both *Formula Books 1* and *2* have been developed from *The Formula Manual* (Stark Research Corporation), a text on the practical application of chemical compounding used by thousands of educational institutions and libraries throughout the world, from elementary through graduate levels.

Stark Research Corporation operates a complete research, development and testing facility where formulas are constantly being modified from large-scale manufacturing quantities to small batches that are suitable for the do-it-yourselfer. New formulas are developed and updated, and all are tested under actual use conditions.

In recognition of the do-it-yourselfer's need for a simple nontechnical approach that doesn't require specialized laboratory equipment such as schools would have, formulas have been chosen that can be made with utensils found in the home. We have also eliminated many technical facets that are important to the student but would not, in all likelihood, be of interest to the consumer.

Many people have helped me immeasurably in the preparation of both *The Formula Book 1, 2,* and in our text edition, *The Formula Manual:* My wife and partner, Eileen, who has been a vital part of our testing program, my daughter Carrie, who makes up formulas and tests them on her 4-H animals, my business partner and secretary, Julie Charnis, who has been a vital ingredient in putting the books together, Jim Andrews of Sheed Andrews and McMeel, whose guidance has been so helpful, Donna Martin, also of Sheed Andrews and McMeel, whose function it is to aid in the organization of the books, and last but certainly not least, Dr. Ed Nigh of the University of Arizona whose technical advice and guidance have been invaluable.

To them, and to the many others who have made suggestions, I say: "Thank you."

—Norman Stark

Introduction

WHY

It has been suggested that *The Formula Manual* and *The Formula Books* 1 and 2 are intended to be an exposé or even an attack on manufacturers of chemical products. Nothing could be further from the truth. Our objective is as follows.

Doing-it-yourself has grown to phenomenal proportions in recent years. In my opinion there are any number of reasons. Two of the most important are (a) the extremely high cost of buying manufactured products or having professional services performed, and (b) the fact that work weeks are getting shorter, providing more time to do-it-yourself.

People in all walks of life are growing their own food, painting their own houses, repairing their own screens, building fences and outbuildings, remodeling, and so forth. But one area where doing-it-yourself has not been generally possible until now is in making your own chemical products. Why?

Suppose you saw an endtable you liked but felt you couldn't afford right now. Because it's a perceptible object you can measure it, copy the size and design, and determine what materials are used in it. And if you have a home workshop, you can probably come up with a pretty close duplicate of it by following instructions in one of the many good books available on furniture making and finishing. On the other hand, chemical products are generally imperceptible in that we can't see what is in them, and to simulate without a formula requires trained people using sophisticated equipment. Therefore, our objective in bringing these books to the market is to give the do-it-yourselfer the option of making his or her own chemical products.

For those of you who flunked high-school chemistry and feel a bit uncomfortable at the thought of playing the sorcerer's apprentice, fear not. If you've ever made pancakes from the recipe off the box then you can follow all instructions in this book with good results. In fact, you might think of this as a recipe book, only you don't eat the results. You use them to keep away mosquitoes, clean your hands, polish your floors, mothproof your clothes, preserve leather, and lots more.

Of course, just as you can buy a finely prepared meal in a restaurant — well, some restaurants at any rate — you can also buy a ready-made cucumber skin lotion or a glass cleaner, for example. But consider what you're paying for besides the ingredients. There's that pretty little can or bottle that it comes in, the packaging that some well-paid designer dreamed up just to catch your eye; there's the cost of distributing it to the retail stores across the country; an advertising budget that would considerably reduce the national debt; and finally, the manufacturer's profit and the retailer's profit. Begin to get the idea?

The reason most of us don't eat all our meals in restaurants is that it's cheaper, more fun, and more satisfying to eat at home. Likewise, I hope that in using this book you experience at least a part of the fun and satisfaction I have had in compiling and testing it.

Many of the recipes are for fairly modern products such as sink disposal cleaner, but there are also a few that are simple old-fashioned ways of doing things that really work. Many old-fashioned methods tend to be forgotten, what with all the fancy stuff for doing the same

Introduction

things on the supermarket shelves. But if the old way works as well or better, and is less expensive, it seems a shame to replace it by something that's more expensive and usually doesn't work any better.

BASIC EQUIPMENT

Most of what you need is probably around the kitchen already, but it's nice to know more or less what you will need before you get started. You may want to duplicate some of your kitchen utensils for this special purpose, and of course, you can improvise. This is a suggested list only. It is handy to have two Pyrex double boilers. Several recipes require heating two separate ingredients in this way, and the glass pots have two advantages: You can see what's going on inside, and they are easy to clean. In addition, a set of large mixing bowls, two or three measuring cups, a standard set of kitchen measuring spoons, and a couple of wooden spoons for mixing and stirring are useful. A plastic cone and filter paper, such as the ones sold for making coffee, can be used to filter small, undissolved particles out of a liquid to make it clearer and prettier, and of course you will need containers for your finished products. Jars, bottles, and cans, all with lids, and plastic squeeze bottles, or anything else you can think of, can be used. Be sure to label all containers, both those holding finished products and those containing raw materials, and keep them well out of the reach of children. A more detailed description of utensils and equipment useful for making the formulas found in *The Formula Book 2* is in Appendix G. Appendix G also contains illustrations of many of these utensils.

RAW MATERIALS AND WHERE TO GET THEM

Chemicals aren't always just chemicals. Some are fairly pure, while others have impurities in them. The pure grades are designated as U.S.P. and the less pure ones are designated either Manufacturing or Technical grade. U.S.P. stands for United States Pharmacopoeia, which means they meet government standards set forth in the U.S.P. book for required purity in chemicals for pharmacological use. Manufacturing or Technical grades have lower standards of purity and are, of course, considerably lower in cost, so they should be used wherever possible. However, if you're using magnesium sulfate (Epsom salts) in something to take internally, for example, you need U.S.P. grade. If you are making something to use as a foot bath or to spray on your plants, then the Technical grade would do as well, depending on how you feel about your feet or your begonias. An extended discussion on the selection of materials is found in Appendix F.

On the subject of alcohol a great deal could be said. There are many different kinds of alcohol that can be made in many different ways for many different purposes. Perhaps the most important fact to remember is that the most common alcohol, called variously ethyl alcohol, ethanol, or grain alcohol, is the only one that can be taken orally, and then only in moderate quantities and diluted by at least an equal amount of water or some other liquid. If you put an "m" in front of it, you get methyl alcohol, called also methanol, or wood alcohol, a violent poison which causes convulsions, blindness, and death. Two other common alcohols, butyl and isopropyl, are only moderately toxic.

Where ethyl alcohol is available for use in beverages for human consumption, it is highly taxed by federal and state governments. Where it is not sold for use in beverages, it is not taxed, and so is much less expensive. But to make sure the alcoholic beverage tax is not evaded, the law requires that ethyl alcohol for nonbeverage uses be adulterated by the addition of some substance which makes it unfit to drink. This adulterated ethyl alcohol is called denatured alcohol. Some of the most common denaturants are benzene, gasoline, kerosene, and methyl alcohol. As a matter of general interest, the types of alcohol and their various uses are described more fully in Appendix E.

Introduction

In almost all cases isopropyl alcohol can be used as a substitute for denatured alcohol. Generally it is less toxic and lower in cost. Your choice should be based on the availability and cost of the two types. Isopropyl alcohol does have an odor which dissipates as it evaporates, leaving the residual odor of the aromatic that's been incorporated in the product. So when testing for the amount of perfume to use, allow about 30 seconds for the isopropyl odor to disappear.

In some applications alcohol is specified to be taken internally, such as in extracts, etc. Here, neither denatured nor isopropyl alcohol can be used. Ethyl alcohol is the only alternative. In many areas this can be purchased from a local liquor store under the name ethyl alcohol, but in other areas you may have to settle for vodka, which is about the same.

The most convenient place to buy your raw materials is at the drugstore. There are several large drug companies with well-known brand names, so pick one in your area, go to the retail outlet, and ask the druggist. If he doesn't have what you need, he can usually either order it for you or tell you where to get it. Walgreen, Rexall, and McKesson are three of the largest and best known drug companies that sell chemicals in small quantities, and if none of them has a retail outlet in your town you may be able to order direct from one of their main offices by getting the address from the label of one of their products. There are also chemical supply companies in most cities. You can check the Yellow Pages of the telephone directory and make a few phone calls to locate what you need. In addition, some petroleum products are best obtained from an oil dealer. Ask at your local service station, or call the office of the oil distributor nearest you.

For the convenience of the reader, a listing of all the chemicals used in *The Formula Book 2* and their usual sources of supply will be found in Appendix I. Following the sources of supply is the number of times that particular chemical is called for in *The Formula Book 2*. This should give the reader some idea, when he finds it necessary to purchase a chemical in a larger quantity than that called for in a particular formula, of how many other uses he can put it to.

SOME HELPFUL HINTS

You may be thinking, "If the smallest amount I can buy is one pound but I only need one ounce, what am I going to do with the rest?" For those of you who think that this might be a problem, we have a couple of suggestions. Nearly all chemicals will keep indefinitely if they are stored in good containers and are protected from moisture, so your one-pound supply can last you two years or twenty, depending on how much is used at a time. With inflation, there is a certain amount of security in knowing that you have, say, a five- or ten-year supply of something. Another excellent idea is to enter into some form of cooperative arrangement with your friends or neighbors. An increasing number of marketing cooperatives are forming across the country, allowing people to buy groceries at wholesale prices and share them among the members of the cooperative. Exactly the same sort of thing could easily be done whenever buying in bulk is necessary. I hasten to add that not all of the products in this book need be bought in bulk. Many of the raw materials you will be using can be bought in small enough quantities to make it reasonable for an individual to produce these things for himself, even on a short-term basis.

A friend of mine once said, with respect to cooking, that whenever she tries a new recipe, she reads it through carefully three times before starting. I have found this to be excellent advice. Don't try to memorize the procedure, but do become familiar with it before you begin.

Although high precision is not required, measurements should be accurate. Teaspoons and tablespoons are level spoonfuls unless otherwise noted. The same is true for cups, half cups, and so on.

Introduction

A "speck" is a measure that is not often used, but it is defined as the amount of material that will lie within a 1/4 inch square marked on a piece of paper or a note card.

If you need to measure, say, 1/3 cup of some lumpy solid material such as paraffin that can't be easily packed into a measuring cup, you might use this method: Fill the cup to the 2/3 cup line with water, then drop in lumps of the material until the water reaches the 1 cup line. The amount of material you have put in will be 1/3 cup. Of course you cannot use this method with a material that is water soluble or that would be difficult to dry.

Eventually we will all have to make an adjustment to the metric system. A detailed explanation of conversion equivalents can be found in Appendix B. Likewise, to give this book an "international" application, Appendix C gives a conversion table from Fahrenheit to Centigrade temperatures.

Many things that are beneficial can also be dangerous when improperly used. Electricity, wired in conformance with a code, is a safe and dependable energy source. But improperly used, it can become a destructive force. Gas is also an important energy source that is safe when properly used. When it is not, it becomes a potentially lethal force. The automobile is a necessary means of transportation which is safe when properly operated, but uncontrolled can be an instrument of death.

Chemicals are no exceptions. Properly used for the purpose they are intended, they contribute a great deal to our life style. But improperly used, they can become a threat to safety. Let's take sodium chloride, ordinary table salt, as an example. Most of us use salt daily in our food, and regard it as a safe chemical. But if a child were to consume large quantities of it, serious consequences could be the result.

In writing *The Formula Book 2*, I have excluded hazardous materials wherever possible, but in some cases they must be included to make a product effective. In making a formula, the reader should observe any note of caution added at the end of the recipe.

The Formula Book 2

In any formulating it is very important to write down *everything* you do. It's so easy to say "Oh, I'll remember that," and then weeks or months later say, "I forgot what I did." And you may want to vary the amount of certain ingredients in a formula. For example, the amount of perfume you put in, or the amount of color that suits you, should be recorded so you can duplicate your results. To encourage the reader to take this important step, note pages have been interspersed throughout the formulas. Please use them.

We all know that materials such as waxes and oils will burn, so I have concentrated the warnings to materials that may be less familiar. These cautionary instructions have been included for your safety in preparation and use of the formulas. The poisonous or toxic characteristics of the chemicals and finished products have been indicated. *Poisonous* is a stronger warning of the danger to human life caused by ingesting these substances than is *toxic*. But remember, all chemicals, including ordinary table salt, should be kept out of the reach of children, carefully labeled, and used only for the purpose they are intended.

And now have fun.

1

Around the House

Around the House

Adhesive Tape Remover

It is estimated that there are over four hundred different types of adhesive tapes for a myriad of uses. Of these, some require that the back be moistened such as in the case of packing tape, while others require no moisture. These are referred to as "pressure sensitive," requiring only pressure to effect adhesion.

Adhesive tape used medicinally for protecting cuts and wounds contains a special adhesive that is free of chemicals that could cause skin irritations. The system is designed in such a way that adhesion is greater to the cloth tape than to the skin, thereby making it easy to remove after it has served its purpose.

Unfortunately the bond is not only to the skin but to the hairs as well, so removal can be a painful process. But here's a formula that will help a lot. (Avoid contact, however, with open lesions.)

You'll need 1/4 cup isopropyl alcohol and 10 drops wintergreen oil extract. Stir the extract into the alcohol and store in a glass eyedropper bottle. To use, apply with dropper along edges of tape and allow fluid to soak in for about 5 minutes before removing. (Caution: Isopropyl alcohol is toxic and flammable.)

Alcohol-Resistant Treatment for Wood

Before holiday preparations leave you time for little else, give your fine wood furniture some preventative maintenance. You'll be glad you did when you're having your Christmas open house or New Year's Eve party and someone spills a drink or leaves a wet glass on a table. Even if you're busy playing host or hostess and don't notice the problem or have the time to attend to it immediately, your furniture won't be damaged by a permanent ring or blemish.

You'll need mineral oil, available from the drugstore, and a little household vinegar. It's so easy.

Mix 1 pint of mineral oil and 2 tablespoons of white

vinegar. Then simply apply with a cloth. It takes a little elbow grease, but you might as well take your frustrations out on your furniture instead of your family. In fact, enlist their help. Polish with a dry cloth. Store excess in a glass or impervious plastic container.

Antiseptic Cleaner — All Purpose

An antiseptic is a substance that stops the growth of bacteria or other microorganisms. There are literally millions of bacteria that inhabit the earth, many good, and some bad.

The "good guys," if we could see them, probably wear white hats. They are not only useful, but some are essential to life. Fertilizer is broken down by bacteria into organic materials that are used by plants. These materials are converted to nutrients that are absorbed by the roots from the soil. Still others live in colonies called nodules, that are attached to the roots of legumes such as alfalfa, clover, and soybeans where they supply essential nitrogen to the plant.

And then there are the "bad guys" with their black hats. These disease producers are parasites that cause all kinds of problems. They are usually found in areas such as bathtubs, showers, toilets, sinks, garbage pails, diaper pails, drains, and other unsavory places where they can be attacked with a vengeance. To do this you need a general purpose antiseptic cleaner. Here's a formula for a good one that you can make easily and inexpensively.

You need 6 cups of trisodium phosphate (TSP), 1 cup sodium carbonate (soda ash), 3/4 cup sodium perborate, 1/4 cup borax, and 2 cups powdered soap (not detergent). Dry mix all ingredients together and store in a glass or impervious plastic container. To use, put 1 cup of mixture into 1 quart hot water, and use for general cleaning. (Caution: TSP is a skin irritant. Use rubber gloves in the preparation and application of cleaner.)

NOTES

Name of Formula: _____

Date Made: _____

Ingredients and amounts: _____

_____

_____

_____

Label: Ingredients and caution warnings

Observations: _____

_____

_____

_____

_____

- - - - - - - - - -

Name of Formula: _____

Date Made: _____

Ingredients and amounts: _____

_____

_____

_____

Label: Ingredients and caution warnings

Observations: _____

_____

_____

_____

_____

NOTES

Name of Formula: _____
Date Made: _____
Ingredients and amounts: _____
_____
_____
_____

Label: Ingredients and caution warnings
Observations: _____
_____
_____
_____
_____

- - - - - - - - - -

Name of Formula: _____
Date Made: _____
Ingredients and amounts: _____
_____
_____
_____

Label: Ingredients and caution warnings
Observations: _____
_____
_____
_____
_____

Around the House

Antistatic Spray for Rugs

Few things are more irritating than to walk across a rug or carpet and get "zapped" by an electric spark when metal, such as a doorknob, is touched. The reason for this happening is that static electricity is built up by the friction between shoe soles and floor coverings. The rubbing disrupts electrons, causing some to leave one substance and enter another. Thus, at least a partial solution to this problem is to reduce the amount of friction, which in turn reduces the amount of static electricity. Here's how to do it.

You'll need 3 tablespoons of silicone oil emulsion and 1 quart of water. (Note: Silicone oil in emulsion form is sometimes difficult to obtain but it's easy to make your own. Measure out 1 cup of the water and add silicone oil and a few drops of a liquid detergent to it. Stir vigorously until oil is dispersed through water, and add this emulsion to balance of water.) Pour into impervious plastic spray bottles and apply to floor covering, especially in heavy traffic areas.

Baking Pan Antistick

Adhesives are great. In our modern society it's hard to imagine how we ever got along without the complex, sophisticated ones we now take for granted. The uses for adhesives are innumerable. Aircraft components are fastened with them, packages are taped shut, building materials are held in place, furniture joints are glued together, the covering on our luggage is attached to the frame, automobile upholstery is held in place, and the books we read are bound with adhesives, just to mention a few of the applications. There's one place where adhesion isn't needed however — that's when baked goods become glued to the pan they're baked in. But there is no need to be stuck (no pun intended) with high priced antistick sprays that don't work any better than one you can make yourself. Here's the formula.

The ingredients you'll need are: 2 tablespoons of soy flour, 6 tablespoons wheat flour, and 1 cup shortening. Cream all ingredients together and store in impervious plastic or glass jar. To use, rub a thin film of the mixture over the pan surface.

Bathtub and Sink Cleaner

Bathtubs and sinks, similar to the types we all know and use, became commonplace in homes with the advent of running water in the early part of the twentieth century. The old-fashioned tubs and sinks were a far cry from the modern fixtures we have in our homes of today.

Sinks and bathtubs are usually made of cast, formed, or in some cases fabricated metal. Then, with the exception of nonrusting metals such as stainless steel, they are coated with an impervious hard glasslike finish such as porcelain. Porcelain enamel is a vitreous material applied to the metal by either spraying or dipping. After this (several coats may be applied), the piece is fired at a temperature of about 1600°F., which causes it to flow and bond to the metal. While bonded porcelain is extremely dense, like glass materials, it does have a degree of porosity. And because bacteria are microorganisms, they can lodge on the surface. For this reason, as well as for cosmetic effect, regular cleaning is essential. Here's an inflation-beater formula that will do a good job.

You'll need 1 cup of trisodium phosphate (TSP), 1 cup powdered soap, and 2 cups calcium carbonate (chalk). Dry mix these ingredients thoroughly and transfer to an open-top jar. To use, pick up this material on a damp cloth or sponge and rub on the surface to be cleaned. Rinse with clear water. Store in glass, impervious plastic or metal containers. (Caution: TSP is a skin irritant. Use rubber gloves in preparation and application of cleaner.)

NOTES

Name of Formula: _____

Date Made: _____

Ingredients and amounts: _____

_____

_____

_____

Label: Ingredients and caution warnings

Observations: _____

_____

_____

_____

_____

- - - - - - - - - -

Name of Formula: _____

Date Made: _____

Ingredients and amounts: _____

_____

_____

_____

Label: Ingredients and caution warnings

Observations: _____

_____

_____

_____

_____

NOTES

Name of Formula: _____
Date Made: _____
Ingredients and amounts: _____
_____
_____
_____

Label: Ingredients and caution warnings
Observations: _____
_____
_____
_____
_____

- - - - - - - - - -

Name of Formula: _____
Date Made: _____
Ingredients and amounts: _____
_____
_____
_____

Label: Ingredients and caution warnings
Observations: _____
_____
_____
_____
_____

Around the House

Blackboard Cleaner

The three R's of education: readin', writin', and 'rithmetic, have been around for a long, long time. And I still feel they are basic. Of my four daughters, three have advanced degrees and I'm sure the fourth will have one in due time. But when a letter comes from one of them — Wow! To decipher what she is saying takes a decoding expert. Whatever happened to the "Palmer" method of penmanship that many of us learned in our educational process?

The blackboard, to me, is a symbol of learning. It can be found in any schoolroom, as well as in industry conference rooms and homes. But when a lesson has been taught, it needs to be erased for the next use. Here's a formula for doing that.

You'll need 2 cups vinegar, 1 cup powdered detergent, and 1 gallon water. Mix the detergent and vinegar into the water. To use, wash blackboard with a sponge or cloth dipped into this solution and rinse with clear water. Then you'll have a "clean slate" for the next lesson.

Carpet Cleaner

When you stop to think about it, carpets can be the reservoir for holding all sorts of dirt and bacteria. This accumulation enters our homes via shoes, boots, and wind, and on the feet and coats of our pets.

We can't live in a sterile void, of course, so our natural body immune system guards us against bacteria up to a certain point. However, since carpets are a holding point for dirt and soil, they can adversely affect allergies, and are a good place to start the clean up.

There are several options. (1) A cleaning service can be called in, (2) cleaning machines can be rented, or (3) you can do it yourself, which is the lowest cost option "by a country mile." If you elect to do it yourself, you'll need 3 cups wheat flour, 1 1/4 cups mineral oil, 1 tablespoon aluminum stearate, 1 tablespoon salicylic acid and

The Formula Book 2

1 3/4 cups water. Mix the flour and water to form a paste, mix the aluminum stearate and salicylic acid into the paste, and then add the mineral oil in a slow stream stirring constantly. Store in glass, metal, or impervious plastic container. To use, brush paste into surface and, after a few minutes, remove with damp cloth or sponge. Do this over sections of the carpet, one at time. (Note: Because there are so many different fibers, test in a small inconspicuous area before cleaning the entire carpet to be sure there will be no discoloration.)

Ceramic Tile Cleaner

Ceramic tile is made from various types of clay and other minerals. The mastic mix (dough) is packed into molds and then fired at high temperatures. In some cases the initial firing may also produce the final finish. However, in others, a finished coat called a frit is fired on the surface of the substrate as a secondary operation.

Frits are made up in liquid form and painted or sprayed on the substrate. These usually contain glass in some form or the other, such as sodium silicates (waterglass) and the color desired for the finished surface. When the piece is fired, the glass softens and the particles flow together forming a dense impervious finish. This is, of course, an oversimplification of the way frits are made. Because of the density of the surface on most ceramic tile, cleaning is not difficult. Here's a formula that's inexpensive to make and will do a good job.

You'll need 2 tablespoons of trisodium phosphate (TSP) and 1 gallon of water. Mix the TSP into the water and wipe over the tile with a sponge dampened in this solution. Store solution in glass or impervious plastic jug. (Caution: TSP is a skin irritant. Use rubber gloves in the preparation and application of the cleaner.)

Christmas Tree Fire Retardant and Needle Preservative

Here's a formula that does double duty — it helps keep your Christmas tree looking good longer while it

Around the House

adds an important safety factor. You'd be well-advised to make up this mix if only to keep your floor from being littered with falling needles. But when you consider that it retards fire, making it becomes a must — especially considering the small amount of time and effort it takes on your part.

You probably already have some of these ingredients on hand in your medicine cabinet and garden supplies, or you can ask for them at your drugstore. Here's what you'll need.

One cup ammonium sulfate, 1/2 cup boric acid, 2 tablespoons borax, and 8 tablespoons hydrogen peroxide (3%). Dissolve all of the above ingredients into 1 gallon hot water. If you want, pine oil emulsion may be added for a longer lasting Christmasy aroma. Transfer some to a spray bottle and spray on the Christmas tree to create a fire-retarding effect. Now, fill the cup in the tree stand with this solution and check every couple of days to make sure the cup is full. It's a good idea to make a fresh cut at the bottom of the trunk to insure that the tree can take in this life-preserving solution. Store in a glass or impervious plastic container.

Coffee Extract

The coffee plant is believed to be a native of Ethiopia, and was introduced into Europe by the Arabs. The plant is a small tree with green leaves and fragrant white flowers. The red fruit is about 1/2" in length containing a yellow pulp encasing two beans. The flavor and aroma of coffee are largely due to the essential oils in the bean.

Extraction is the procedure of separating a selected material from the other materials contained in a mass. There are two principal processes for accomplishing this: (1) mechanical extraction, or (2) solvent extraction. For our purposes here, the solvent method is used.

You'll need 1/8 cup finely ground coffee and 1/2 cup ethyl alcohol. (Note: Ethyl alcohol, sometimes called grain alcohol, 100 proof, is available in most liquor stores, but if it is not, 90 proof vodka may be substituted.) The easiest apparatus to use is a plastic coffee cone and coffee filter paper. Place the cone and filter paper over a glass jar and put in the ground coffee. Next, pour 1/2 of the alcohol or vodka (1/4 cup) over the coffee. Wait until dripping stops and pour the remainder of the alcohol over the coffee. The extract, now in the jar, may be poured over the grounds several more times for greater strength. Transfer extract to well-sealed glass or impervious plastic bottles to prevent evaporation. Label and store out of reach of children. (We don't want any "tipsy tots" staggering around the kitchen.) Use for flavoring and aromatic effect in foods.

Dance Floor Wax

Have you made your plans for New Year's Eve? A party at home, including dancing on a well-waxed floor, would be an inexpensive and delightful way to welcome in the New Year. Most of us, from youngsters to oldsters, enjoy dancing to our own style of music, whether it be square, swing, or rock. The needs are simple: friends, music, and a good dance floor.

If you have a smooth-surfaced floor in your recreation room, basement, or on your patio, it is not necessary to spend a month's entertainment money to dance at a club or a hotel. Here is the formula to help you wax your floor. Then invite your friends — turn up your stereo and dance.

The ingredients required are 1 cup of stearic acid, which may be purchased from a candle supply or hobby shop, and 1/2 pound of talc, available from a ceramic supply house. Mix the two thoroughly and sprinkle the mixture on the floor. Store in glass, paper, or impervious plastic container.

NOTES

Name of Formula: _____

Date Made: _____

Ingredients and amounts: _____

_____

_____

_____

Label: Ingredients and caution warnings

Observations: _____

_____

_____

_____

_____

- - - - - - - - - -

Name of Formula: _____

Date Made: _____

Ingredients and amounts: _____

_____

_____

_____

Label: Ingredients and caution warnings

Observations: _____

_____

_____

_____

_____

NOTES

Name of Formula: _____

Date Made: _____

Ingredients and amounts: _____

_____

_____

_____

Label: Ingredients and caution warnings

Observations: _____

_____

_____

_____

_____

- - - - - - - - - -

Name of Formula: _____

Date Made: _____

Ingredients and amounts: _____

_____

_____

_____

Label: Ingredients and caution warnings

Observations: _____

_____

_____

_____

_____

Around the House

Fire Extinguishing Powder

Many things that we regard as being essential to our way of life can become instruments of death and destruction when out of control. It's hard to imagine our society functioning without automobiles, trucks, and aircraft. Under control, these marvelous machines contribute greatly to our way of life, but out of control they can be lethal.

Combustion is the basic energy that runs our nation. It fuels our vehicles, makes our electricity, heats and cools our homes, produces materials that make our manufactured products possible, and helps to supply our food. But when it gets out of control, billions of dollars of losses occur and thousands of lives are needlessly lost. It is said that an ounce of prevention is worth a pound of cure. Here are some things we all can do to lessen our risk from fire.

Fire departments and other municipal agencies, as well as insurance companies, have a great stake in fire prevention. Their expert knowledge is invaluable and available to anyone. Call on them for advice. They are in a position to point out potentially dangerous situations and how to correct them, and will assure you that fire extinguishers, strategically placed, are essential. Here's a simple formula for a low cost, easily made fire extinguisher powder.

You'll need 6 pounds of fine silica mason sand that you can get from any building supply dealer, and 2 pounds of sodium bicarbonate from the grocery store. Dry mix the two materials thoroughly and store in 1 pound (glass, metal, or impervious plastic) containers in strategic locations. To use, sprinkle directly on base of flame to smother fire.

Fireplace Flame Colors

When you gather around the fireplace this holiday season (or any winter evening) you can make the fire more interesting and fascinating by adding color to the flames. It's easy and inexpensive to do.

Dry mix 1 cup of calcium chloride (if you have trouble getting this, state, county, and city highway shops stock it for ice and dust control), 1 cup borax, and 1 cup sodium chloride (ordinary table salt) in a bowl. The calcium chloride produces an orange color, the borax green, and the salt yellow. Of course you may prefer only a single color in which case you would use only that material. Sprinkle either material or mixture on the logs. Or, you may want to drill some holes in the yule log and fill it with the material for a longer lasting effect. Store excess in glass or impervious plastic containers.

Fireplace Flue Soot Remover

Fireplace smoke should go up the chimney not in the house. But unfortunately this is not always the case. A frequent cause is a buildup of carbon deposits (soot) on the surfaces of the flue. Here's a simple, low cost way to reduce this buildup.

Dry mix 1 cup of sodium chloride (ordinary table salt) with 1 cup of powdered zinc oxide, available from most drugstores. Sprinkle 1 cup of this mixture on a hot fire. After about 5 minutes, distribute the balance on the logs. Store excess in glass or impervious plastic container. (Caution: Zinc oxide is highly poisonous.)

Fire Retardant Paper

It is contended by many historians that paper was first made by the Chinese about 300 B.C. I disagree. The common wasp was making it long before that. We've all seen wasps' nests hanging from eaves of buildings. And I for one have, on occasion, observed a little too closely. Ouch! The wasp collects wood fiber and actually builds a compartmented home, the walls of which are genuine paper.

Around the House

Modern papermaking is a highly sophisticated science, producing the finished product at speeds of up to 500 feet per minute, or even more in some cases. There are many different kinds of paper, depending on the end use. But all have a manufacturing method in common. Fibers, whether they be cotton, jute, hemp, flax, grass, straw, or wood are digested to a fine mass and then formed into webs. This is of course an oversimplification of a highly complex art.

Fire retardancy can be built into paper during the manufacturing process by the addition of chemical additives. However, there are many uses for paper where this is not needed and would only increase the cost. So if you want to use paper in areas where fires could be a hazard, such as in decorations, for example, you can help provide this protection yourself. Here's an easy economical way to deter paper from supporting combustion.

You'll need 1 cup of ammonium sulfate (from any garden shop), 6 tablespoons boric acid (from any druggist), 4 tablespoons borax (from a grocer), and 3 cups water (from your friendly sink). Dissolve the first three ingredients into the water while stirring. To use, apply to paper surface with brush or plastic spray bottle and dry. Store excess in a glass, metal, or impervious plastic container.

General Purpose Deodorant and Disinfectant

Bacteria and fungi are everywhere, so even the most meticulously kept home harbors millions of them. It's a paradox that some are harmful, causing disease and property destruction, while others are highly beneficial, and even edible.

There are areas around any home that are favorite gathering spots. Fungi, such as mold for example, seem to thrive in damp areas, and harmful bacteria in garbage cans, sinks, bathtubs, shower stalls, and decomposed food. But because they can be anywhere it seems sensible to use an all-purpose cleaner that has antiseptic qualities for general cleaning purposes. Here's the formula.

The Formula Book 2

You'll need 1 pint of pine oil, 1/2 pound powdered soap and 1 pint water. Gently stir the soap into the water mixing slowly. Remove suds from surface of liquid. Now pour in the pine oil very slowly stirring constantly. To use, dilute solution with water or use full strength depending on job to be done. Store in glass, metal, or impervious plastic container.

Grass Stain Remover

Chlorophyll is the substance that makes grass green. It is so important that without it, no life could exist. Chlorophyll, in combination with sun and air, makes it possible for plants to manufacture their own food which in turn feeds people and animals. It is a highly complex substance made up of carbon, hydrogen, magnesium, nitrogen, and oxygen.

In spite of its miracles, chlorophyll has one drawback. When junior is making like the great Henry Aaron sliding into third base, it can do a very efficient job of depositing grass stains on his T-shirt. But there is a simple inexpensive way to get rid of the stains — pronto. All you need is to mix 1 1/2 cups of isopropyl alcohol (91%) with 1/2 cup water. Before putting the textile in the washing machine, soak the spot in this mixture for a few minutes and rub away the stain. Store in glass or impervious plastic container. (Caution: Isopropyl alcohol is mildly toxic and flammable.)

Heating or Cooling Filter Cleaning Compound

Furnace filters are essential to the operation of a recirculating heating/cooling system. Their function is to trap dust, dirt, and pollen before they infiltrate the building. While filters do decrease the airflow, the manufacturer of the equipment has taken this into account and has sized the blower to compensate for it.

When the pressure drop, i.e., the amount of air passing over the filter, reaches a point where insufficient air

Around the House

is passing through the system, the filters have done their job and are plugged with dirt. And now it's time to do something about it. There are two alternatives: (1) the old filter can be discarded and a new disposable one put in, which will make the filter manufacturer happy, or (2) the old filter can be cleaned, which will make your budget happy. If your choice is the latter, use this formula to clean your old filter and make it as good as new.

You'll need 1 teaspoon of sodium metasilicate, 1 teaspoon of liquid detergent, and 1 quart of water. Mix these ingredients together and brush on dirty filter. Allow to soak for about 30 minutes and flush with garden hose and clear water to remove dirt. Reinstall filter and repeat cleaning process as necessary. Store excess in glass or impervious plastic container.

Ice Cube Release

Maybe you're having a party. You have on your cocktail dress and the snacks are laid out on the table. Then the guests arrive. Now you take drink orders, soft or hard, and they all need ice. But you're ready because you've frozen ice cubes ahead of time. But are you? First you turn the cube trays over the sink. Nothing happens. Then you hit the tray against the sink. Again nothing. Finally you try hot water, and then they come out, much smaller than they should be. This can be avoided.

All you need is 2 tablespoons corn oil and 2 tablespoons peanut oil. Mix these two ingredients together and coat inside of ice cube trays and dividers before putting in water. Store mixture in glass or impervious plastic containers.

Library Paste

What parents haven't been proud when their child brings home a paper cherry tree, Easter bunny, an eerie witch or pumpkin face, pilgrims with a wild turkey, or a

Santa Claus face? Credit must be given to those dedicated people, their teachers, who instill creativeness at an early age. It will undoubtedly have an effect on their entire adult lives.

Aside from the other materials, library paste plays an important part in "pasting it all together." But there are also many other uses outside the classroom for this inexpensive and easy to make adhesive. Here's the way to make your own library paste.

All you will need is 1/2 cup cornstarch, 3/4 cup cold water, and 6 cups boiling water. Make a paste of the cornstarch and cold water. Add this paste to the boiling water and stir until a translucent mixture forms. Cool down to room temperature and store in glass or impervious plastic containers. To use, coat a thin film on the surface to be bonded and apply pressure until bond forms.

Liquid Porcelain Cleaner

Getting off the scum that forms on the sink, bathtub, and shower enclosure becomes a problem. Here's an inexpensive formula for you to use on those fixtures.

You'll need 1 cup mineral oil (lowest cost grade) and 1 cup deodorized kerosene. Mix ingredients together and store in an impervious plastic or glass jar. To use, dampen cloth with solution and rub over surface. Rinse with clear water. (Caution: Kerosene is flammable and toxic. Do not use near open flame. Use rubber gloves, or wash hands thoroughly with soap and water after use.)

Lubricating Stick

Of life's little annoyances, one that tops my list is things that stick when they're not supposed to. A drawer that resists being pulled open, a window that won't go up or down as it was made to do, the car door that squeaks when it's closed, the key that has to be forcibly pushed into and pulled out of the lock, these are just a few examples. The cause? Friction.

Around the House

Friction can be broadly defined as the resistance between two surfaces that move against each other. As friction increases, the energy required to produce the movement increases as well. A good example is an electric motor rotating a shaft inside a fixed bearing. The resistance (friction) between the surface of the shaft and the face of the bearing has a direct effect on the amount of energy the motor is required to supply to turn the shaft. The antidote? Lubrication.

There are many different types of lubricants such as oils, greases, silicones, waxes, and graphite. For the applications mentioned, I prefer lubricating sticks because of the low cost and ease of application. You can make them easily and inexpensively. Here's the formula.

Before you begin formulating you'll need to make up some paper tubes and molds. I find a convenient size to be about 3/8" in diameter and 4" long. These can be rolled from ordinary wrapping paper and tied or taped around the circumference to hold the paper in place. One end of the tube must be taped or stapled closed.

Measure out 1/2 cup petrolatum (Vaseline or equivalent) and 1/2 cup paraffin wax. Put both ingredients in the top of a double boiler (never over direct heat) and warm until melted. Mix and allow to cool to just above the solidification point. Pour into paper tubes and let stand until solid. To use, peel off paper from closed end and apply lubricant, with rubbing action, to surface where friction is to be reduced.

Mildewproofing for Book Bindings

Mildew is one of the more than 250,000 known fungi. Of these only mushrooms and truffles are edible. Fungi are essential to our ecology system, converting organic matter back into the soil as compost does. And, of course, one of mankind's greatest lifesavers, penicillin, was discovered initially by the action of fungi on grain. But there are two sides to every coin, so let's take a look at the other side.

The Formula Book 2

Mildew doesn't seem to understand what it should or should not attack, and therein lies the problem. Bookbindings made of organic materials are a favorite target. But there is an easy inexpensive way to combat this scourge. Here's how to do it.

You'll need 1/4 ounce of copper sulfate (see caution warnings at the end of instructions), 1 pint of water, and a piece of soft flannel cloth. Dissolve the copper sulfate in the water and stir. Dip cloth into solution and wring semidry. (Note: Wash your hands thoroughly after doing this.) Dry cloth in moderate heat, laying it on a piece of paper toweling which should later be discarded. Identify cloth with a felt marker as containing poison. (Caution: Copper sulfate is poisonous and must be handled carefully. Dispose of all excess solution after cloth has been impregnated.) To use, rub cloth lightly over book cover. One application will last for many months depending on the amount of humidity in the air. (Caution: If you have small children or dogs, especially puppies, who might chew on books, avoid treatment of books they might come into contact with.)

Moth Repellent

When it's time to pack away woolens for the spring and summer months, they should be protected by a good moth repellent. Those pesky critters can go through a wardrobe leaving nothing but chewed up possessions. When the time comes to wear that favorite sweater (perhaps a Christmas present) it may be a see-through style because the moths found it a favorite, too. Here's a simple, inexpensive way to protect your woolens.

Cut cardboard strips about 2" x 4" and punch a hole near the center of the top edge. Now you'll need 1 pound of paradichlorobenzene (don't let this eight-cylinder word scare you. Ask for moth crystals at your hardware store and you'll have it). Put the paradichlorobenzene in the top of a double boiler (the amount depends on how many cards you plan to coat) and turn on heat. When the ma-

Around the House

terial has melted dip the cards into it repeatedly, allowing to cool between each dip, until a coating of about 1/4" has built up on each side of the card. (Caution: Paradichlorobenzene is moderately toxic by ingestion and vapors are irritating to eyes. Melt in well-ventilated area such as under a stove exhaust fan.) Store excess material in airtight glass or impervious plastic jar. (Caution: Both the ingredients and cards should be carefully stored and kept out of the reach of children.)

Oil and Grease Spot Remover

If you stop to think about it, oils and grease are materials that we are all exposed to in our daily lives. When we get up in the morning, after our shower or bath, some of us may apply an oil-based hair dressing, use an oil-based skin cream, or apply an oil-based dressing or polish to our shoes. Then at breakfast we may have butter or margarine with our toast or to fry our eggs. And we may then wisely check the oil level in the car before using it for the day. At lunchtime we may have mayonnaise on our sandwich, or oil and vinegar dressing on our salad. And when we get home again after the day's work, we might have an anchovy, sardine, or piece of herring on a cracker, with a cocktail before dinner.

With all this exposure to oil and grease, it's a pretty good bet that some of it will find a way to spot our clothes. And if it does, here's a simple and inexpensive way to get rid of the spots.

You'll need 1 cup of diatomaceous earth. This is a commonly used material in swimming pool filters and can be obtained from a pool supply dealer or a ceramic shop.

To use, sprinkle the material on the oil or grease spot and allow about 15 minutes for it to absorb the oil. Then brush the material off the surface. Store excess material in glass, metal, or impervious plastic container.

The Formula Book 2

Paint and Wall Cleaner

Painted walls and woodwork take a lot of abuse that makes cleaning necessary, the frequency depending on the amount of wear and tear they're subjected to. Dirt and dust in the air, cooking vapors, smudges from little hands, cigar, cigarette, and pipe smoke all contribute their share.

The paint used for trim usually differs from that used on walls. While there are exceptions of course, trim is usually painted with enamel and flat paint is used for wall surfaces. Enamel is basically oil paint with clear varnish added. It produces a dense hard surface that is quite resistant to dirt and vapor absorption. Flat wall paint, whether it be oil or water based, has a lower density and greater porosity than enamel and as such is likely to need cleaning more frequently. Here's a formula to produce an economical cleaner that will handle trim enamel or flat paint equally well.

You'll need 1 cup soda ash (sodium carbonate) and 1 tablespoon ammonium sulfate. Dry mix these two ingredients and store in a glass or plastic container. To use, mix 2 tablespoons of powder in 1 gallon hot water and wash surface with a sponge. Note: Strength of solution is governed by condition of surface to be cleaned. Rubber gloves are recommended when a strong solution is used. Store loosely in glass or impervious plastic containers. Do not store in airtight containers, as pressure might build up.

Range Cleaner and Polish

With the possible exception of the new flush heating surfaces on some stoves, ranges of today seem to be just about as hard to clean as they were years ago. My wife and partner Eileen can recall her mother's exasperation over cleaning a stove top and I can do the same. As a matter of fact, before writing this formula, I talked to a number of homemakers and home economists who share these views.

Around the House

While it's true, of course, that many advances have been made, such as timers and variable heat settings, the cleaning problem seems to remain. It's out of my area of expertise to suggest a solution; however, I can provide a formula for a cleaner that may make the job a little less irksome, and save you some money to boot.

You'll need 1/4 cup trisodium phosphate (TSP), 1/4 cup soda ash, and 1/2 cup sodium perborate. Dry mix these three ingredients together in a bowl with a fork. Store in glass or impervious plastic jars. To use: Pick up powder on a damp sponge or cloth and rub over soiled areas. Remove dirt with a wet cloth soaked in clear water. (Caution: TSP is a skin irritant. Use rubber gloves in preparation and application of polish.)

Refrigerator Deodorant

In these days of staggering food prices and hungry people around the world, waste should not be tolerated. This means that leftovers should be saved and used again for another meal. But this does present a problem in that the morning glass of milk that one of the kids didn't drink can absorb the garlic odor from the excess meatballs of last night's dinner — both stored in the same refrigerator.

Obviously what is needed is an odor-absorbing substance that will contain the scents so they won't intermingle. After all, we can't blame a kid for not wanting to drink "garlic milk." So here's an effective low-cost way to prevent the problem.

You'll need 1 cup portland cement, 1/4 cup silica gel (any refrigeration serviceman will have this), 1/4 cup chalk, and 1 cup vermiculite. Mix these ingredients thoroughly and add sufficient water to form a creamlike paste. This mixture may then be poured into molds, which can be made from paper boxes or metal cans, and allowed to dry at about 300°F. in an oven. To use, place molded block in refrigerator. After several weeks of use, remove and reactivate by putting in oven for 3 to 4 hours at 400°F., after which it may be reused.

The Formula Book 2

Sink Disposal Cleaner

You can buy a number of different brands of cleaners for sink disposals — all at fancy prices. Or you can make this simple concoction that works very well, at a fraction of the cost.

Mix 1 cup of vinegar in a sufficient amount of water to fill an ice-cube tray. Freeze the mixture. Now start your disposal and feed the cubes into it to be ground. After the grinding action has stopped, flush with *cold* water for a minute or so.

The principle here is an interesting one. Many fats, such as butter for example, are semisolid at room temperature and in this state will cling to surfaces. The cold temperature of the ice tends to solidify the fats, and permits the vinegar and abrasion of the ground ice to remove the fat deposits.

Soapless Rug Cleaner

Even if you have wall-to-wall carpeting, many folks like throw rugs put in strategic high-traffic areas over the carpeting. And for this very reason, the rugs take quite a beating.

Of course, you can send them out to a cleaner and pay the price if you've a mind to, or you can clean them yourself and "save a bundle" if you're so inclined. If so, here's a formula that I find works well.

You'll need 1 cup isopropyl alcohol, 5 cups white vinegar and 1/4 teaspoon lauryl pyridinium chloride. Mix the alcohol and vinegar together and stir in the lauryl pyridinium chloride until dissolved. Store in impervious plastic or glass bottles. To use, brush mixture into surface of rug, let dry and remove residue with vacuum cleaner. (Note: Because there are so many different fibers, test in a small inconspicuous area to be sure there will be no discoloration.)

NOTES

Name of Formula: _____

Date Made: _____

Ingredients and amounts: _____
_____
_____
_____

Label: Ingredients and caution warnings

Observations: _____
_____
_____
_____
_____

- - - - - - - - - -

Name of Formula: _____

Date Made: _____

Ingredients and amounts: _____
_____
_____
_____

Label: Ingredients and caution warnings

Observations: _____
_____
_____
_____
_____

NOTES

Name of Formula: _____

Date Made: _____

Ingredients and amounts: _____

_____

_____

_____

Label: Ingredients and caution warnings

Observations: _____

_____

_____

_____

_____

_____

- - - - - - - - - -

Name of Formula: _____

Date Made: _____

Ingredients and amounts: _____

_____

_____

_____

Label: Ingredients and caution warnings

Observations: _____

_____

_____

_____

_____

Around the House

Vinyl Cleaner

Polyvinyl materials have found wide applications in the home and in industry. They frequently replace natural materials such as leather and are found in furniture coverings, automobile tops, decorative wall coverings, floors, luggage, and many other applications too numerous to mention. The art of manufacture has become so sophisticated that it's sometimes hard to tell vinyl from leather. But if you're ever stumped there's a simple test that can be made. Wet a small area on the surface. If the dampened area produces a slight odor — it's leather, if not it's synthetic. So the next time "Honest Al," your friendly used car salesman, talks about leather upholstery, you can check him on the spot.

Because it's highly impervious, vinyl is easy to clean with little effort and at low cost. Simply dry mix 1 cup calcium carbonate (chalk) and 3 cups bicarbonate of soda. To use, sprinkle mix on damp sponge or cloth and rub over vinyl surface. Remove with damp cloth and clear water.

Wallpaper Remover

Adhesion is caused by a strong attraction between molecules of dissimilar substances in contact with each other. Wallpaper, attached to a different surface such as a plastered wall, demonstrates this principle.

Wallpaper, at least in my opinion, is an excellent decorating material. The almost endless varieties of colors, designs, and textures make it far more versatile than paint, and it seems to have a warmth that a painted surface doesn't have. But even the best grades do get worn and dirty in time, or you may just get bored with the same pattern and color year after year and want to replace it. Now comes the problem of breaking the adhesion so it can be removed.

To make a good inexpensive wallpaper remover you'll need 1/2 cup liquid detergent, 2 cups of water and

The Formula Book 2

1/2 cup ethylene glycol monoethyl ether. Mix the three materials together. To use, mix 1/2 cup of the concentrate into 1 quart of hot water and apply to wallpaper with sponge. Allow to soak for 10 minutes or so and remove with a scraper. Store in glass or impervious plastic container. (Caution: Ethylene glycol monoethyl ether is flammable and toxic by ingestion.)

Water Softener — All Purpose

It's almost impossible to get anything really clean in hard water. Soap scum forms and lodges in fabrics, or streaks dishes and glassware. Water hardness varies greatly in different areas. In some sections water is as soft as rain, while in others it's hard as iron. Hardness is caused principally by dissolved salts. Softeners that treat the entire home supply usually work on an ion exchange system where a resin has the capacity to exchange the sodium for other salts such as magnesium, and do a good job. However, many homes do not have central softening systems, and here it's necessary to treat individual supplies such as in a dishpan, washing machine, etc. Perhaps this would apply to that summer cabin at the lake, the house trailer, mobile van, or on camping trips.

One of the unusual materials available for the formulators' use is our old friend sodium silicate (waterglass). Among its many uses, it also will soften water, when combined with sodium carbonate (soda ash). Here's the formula for an easy to make and inexpensive water softener.

You'll need 6 cups sodium silicate (waterglass) and 3 cups sodium carbonate (soda ash). Mix the two materials thoroughly and store in a glass or impervious plastic container. To use, mix this concentrate into water at the rate of about 1/2 teaspoon to 5 gallons. (Note: Because water hardness varies greatly, you'll have to experiment as to the amount to use for your locality.)

Around the House

Wood Floor Bleach II

Wood is a beautiful material. It has a feeling of warmth that many other materials don't have. A well-kept wood floor enhances the beauty of any home. But it must be properly cared for to be at its best. One of the major problems is discoloration. Dirt and stains can become ground in, causing unsightly darkening. When this happens, bleaching is called for. However, advance preparation is essential.

Accumulations of wax, oil, and dirt must be removed. The best and most economical way I have found to do this is to use ordinary washing soda and very hot water. About a cup of soda to a gallon of water seems about right. Scrub the floor thoroughly and rinse with clear water. You're now ready to apply the bleach. Here's the formula.

You'll need 1/2 pound of sodium perborate and cold water. Mix sufficient water into the sodium perborate to make a paste of a brushable consistency. Spread paste on floor, working in one section at a time, and allow to stand and "work" for about 30 minutes. Remove with clear water. Repeat this procedure as often as necessary to bring surface to the degree of lightness you desire. (Caution: Because the materials you will use can be irritating to the skin, rubber gloves are suggested.) Store the excess in a glass or impervious plastic container.

NOTES

Name of Formula: _____

Date Made: _____

Ingredients and amounts: _____

_____

_____

_____

Label: Ingredients and caution warnings

Observations: _____

_____

_____

_____

_____

- - - - - - - - -

Name of Formula: _____

Date Made: _____

Ingredients and amounts: _____

_____

_____

_____

Label: Ingredients and caution warnings

Observations: _____

_____

_____

_____

_____

NOTES

Name of Formula: _____

Date Made: _____

Ingredients and amounts: _____

_____

_____

_____

Label: Ingredients and caution warnings

Observations: _____

_____

_____

_____

_____

- - - - - - - - - -

Name of Formula: _____

Date Made: _____

Ingredients and amounts: _____

_____

_____

_____

Label: Ingredients and caution warnings

Observations: _____

_____

_____

_____

_____

2
Personal

The Formula Book 2

Caution

In those formulas in which it is felt that there is a possibility of allergic reaction, it is suggested that the formulas be applied to a small test area to determine if an allergic reaction takes place and if it does, use should be discontinued. However, if the reader or user of the formula is prone to allergic reactions, all personal products should be tested in this way.

It is also suggested that all containers and mixing utensils for personal care formulas, especially those used near the eyes, should be sterilized or at least thoroughly washed.

Personal

Antiperspirant Foot Powder

Perspiration is an enemy of feet. It causes a cold clammy feeling, and the bacteria and fungi, always present, cause odors and destroy shoe leather.

Perspiration is a natural and essential function in the human body. Its purpose is to eliminate wastes, and to control body temperature by evaporation much as a mechanical refrigeration system does. But when this perspiration is contained, as it often is in shoes, it ceases to retain its function and problems appear. And then, the solution to these problems are to reduce the amount of perspiration to an acceptable level by an antiperspirant. Here's a formula that has been successful in doing that.

Dry mix 1 tablespoon powdered alum with 1/4 cup boric acid, and 1/3 cup talc. To use, sprinkle on feet, especially between toes and in shoes. Store in a glass or impervious plastic container.

Astringent Skin Cream

While this formula is not really difficult to make, it is somewhat more complex than previous ones have been. As we all know, oil and water will not mix. So to combine them we need to form an emulsion, that is, to disperse the oil droplets throughout the mixture so they are held in suspension.

An astringent is a material that contracts the tissues of the skin causing a tightening effect. In this formula, powdered alum is the ingredient that accomplishes this function.

You'll need 2 cups white mineral oil, 1/2 cup white beeswax, 1 1/2 tablespoons borax, 2 tablespoons powdered alum and 1 cup water. All containers and mixing utensils for this formula should be sterilized or at least thoroughly washed.

Heat the mineral oil and beeswax together in the top of a double boiler (never over an open flame) until the beeswax is melted and mixed with the mineral oil, then cool down to 120°F. Now in a separate pan, heat water to 120°F. and stir in borax and powdered alum, mixing until dissolved. Next, pour this mixture slowly into the mixture of mineral oil and beeswax stirring constantly. When the final mixture has cooled down to just above the solidification point a few drops of oil-soluble perfume may be added as desired. Store in glass or impervious plastic jars. Use this cream to smooth and firm skin on face and neck and around elbows — and ankles. Note: While these are gentle ingredients in the quantities stated, some people do have allergies. It is therefore suggested that the cream be applied to a small test area to determine if an allergic reaction takes place. If it does, use should be discontinued.

Baby Oil II

A baby's cry at night means "get here on the double" and moms and pops do exactly that. As a matter of fact, when our children were babies, I have seen their mother jump out of bed seconds before the cry was heard. Talk about ESP.

Some of the most common causes of skin discomfort (assuming it is not of a clinical nature which only the doctor is qualified to diagnose and treat), are dryness and irritation. Frequent bathing, even with the mildest soaps, removes natural oils which should be replaced. And replacing the oils serves another important purpose in that these oils act as a barrier to help in preventing excrements from irritating the delicate skin. Of course, you should get advice from your pediatrician and if he recommends baby oil, here's a formula that can save you a bundle.

You'll need 2 tablespoons of almond oil, 8 tablespoons of olive oil (best grade of purity), and a few drops of perfume, if desired. Thoroughly mix all ingredients and store in glass or impervious plastic bottles.

NOTES

Name of Formula: _____

Date Made: _____

Ingredients and amounts: _____

_____

_____

_____

Label: Ingredients and caution warnings

Observations: _____

_____

_____

_____

_____

- - - - - - - - - -

Name of Formula: _____

Date Made: _____

Ingredients and amounts: _____

_____

_____

_____

Label: Ingredients and caution warnings

Observations: _____

_____

_____

_____

_____

NOTES

Name of Formula: _____

Date Made: _____

Ingredients and amounts: _____

_____

_____

_____

Label: Ingredients and caution warnings

Observations: _____

_____

_____

_____

_____

- - - - - - - - - -

Name of Formula: _____

Date Made: _____

Ingredients and amounts: _____

_____

_____

_____

Label: Ingredients and caution warnings

Observations: _____

_____

_____

_____

_____

Personal

Baby Powder

Talc (also known as soapstone or steatite) is the softest of all minerals. It occurs in the ground in the form of thin-flaked sheets or in chunk form, from which it may be ground to a powder.

Two causes of skin irritation in babies are friction and excrements. Talc has an oily, slippery feel that makes it ideal as an antifriction agent helpful in reducing irritation. And because it is acidproof, and urine contains acids, it is an excellent barrier against irritation caused by acids. Here's how to make your own baby powder.

You'll need 2 cups of talc (U.S.P. Grade) and a few drops of oil soluble perfume, if you want the powder scented. Mix the two thoroughly and store in glass, metal, or impervious plastic shaker cans. (Note: U.S.P. means United States Pharmacopeia, which prescribes standards of purity established by the Federal Government.) Caution: Do not use baby powder where a respiratory problem exists or against doctor's advice.

Ballpoint Ink Remover for Hands

The ballpoint pen has largely replaced the fountain pen as a writing tool. While fluid ink is still produced in vast quantities, its use is now primarily in the printing industry.

Some of you readers who have lived through "many summers," as I have, will recall that when the ballpoint pen was first introduced it created a sensation. At that time it cost $15.00 and now it can be bought for as little as 19¢. It's sort of nice to see a price go down, isn't it?

Along with the decline of fluid writing ink, the blotter has also largely disappeared. So when a pen point picks up lint from the paper, another source for removing it needs to be found. In many cases this turns out to be our fingers. If you encounter this as I do, here's an easy inexpensive way to remove the stains from hands.

Into 3 tablespoons of isopropyl alcohol, mix 1 tablespoon glycerin. To use, dip cloth in solution and rub away the spot. Store in glass or impervious plastic container. (Caution: Isopropyl alcohol is mildly toxic and flammable.)

Bay Rum

It is claimed that bay rum was first made by the West Indies natives who prepared it by distilling rum to which bay leaves had been added.

Bay rum is widely used for cosmetic purposes by barbers, beauticians, and for home use as a hair dressing and after shave lotion. The alcohol content tends to disinfect minor shaving nicks and provides a cooling sensation due to evaporation.

You'll need 1/2 teaspoon lemon extract, 1 teaspoon orange extract, 2 cups vodka or isopropyl alcohol, 1 tablespoon glycerin, 2 cups water, and bay leaves to suit. Mix the first four ingredients into the water. Stir well and add bay leaves. Bottle in glass or impervious plastic containers and allow to steep until perfume is at proper strength for your preference. Use as desired.

(Note: If isopropyl alcohol is used a slight odor will be detected. However, when exposed to air, it will dissipate in about 30 seconds allowing the odors of the aromatics to come through.)

Beauty Clay

Beauty clay is probably as old as cosmetics themselves. I've read somewhere that Cleopatra splashed river mud on her skin as a beauty aid. Whether it did any good or not is unknown. She did have a way with the boys however. So who knows?

Many women travel to beauty spas where the mud is supposed to have skin-rejuvenating powers. Again, who knows? But it's my guess that any material such as mud or clay has a "drawing effect" when it dries, just like the poultice that grandma used to slap on our chests when we caught a bad cold.

Personal

So before you spend $20.00 or $30.00 for a beauty-clay facial at your local salon, why not try this formula for about 10¢ per treatment. But remember, if you land a job as a model or movie star, I'll expect a royalty.

All containers and mixing utensils for this formula should be sterilized or at least thoroughly washed. The materials you need are 2 1/2 pounds of powdered clay, 1/8 cup tincture of benzoin, and water. Mix the tincture of benzoin into the clay. (Note: A flour sifter is excellent for this and will also remove lumps and foreign matter.) Store mixture in glass, impervious plastic, paper, or metal container. To use: Take about a cup of this mixture and add water slowly with constant stirring until a thick creamlike consistency results. Paint this mixture to about 1/8" thickness on face with a soft brush. Allow to dry for about an hour and wash off with clear water.

Blackhead Remover

Skin is the largest organ of the human body. Its functions are to protect, send impulses to the brain (when you touch a hot surface the pain triggers the brain which in turn signals the muscles to pull the finger away from the source of pain), excrete waste and act to control body temperature.

The skin surface consists of many pores which are conduits for the flow of perspiration. In addition, they hold oils that are supplied by the sebaceous glands directly below its surface. As the oil becomes contaminated by dirt and oxidation, it turns dark in color and forms what we call blackheads.

Blackheads can be removed in several ways, or by a combination of them: (1) frequently, when pressure is applied by the fingers on each side of the pore, its accumulation can be discharged; (2) a solvent material can be applied, softening the content so it can be washed away; (3) or a combination of methods can be used, which is by far the most effective.

The Formula Book 2

Here's an easy way to make up the softener, simply and effectively. You'll need 1 teaspoon triethanolamine, 2 tablespoons glycerin, 1 3/4 cups isopropyl alcohol and 3 cups water. Mix the isopropyl alcohol into the water. Next, mix in the glycerin and finally stir in the triethanolamine. To use, apply to skin at night and remove by washing in the morning. Any stubborn areas will be easy to remove by pressure since the accumulated deposits will have been softened. Store softener in glass or impervious plastic container. (Caution: Isopropyl alcohol is mildly toxic and flammable.)

Callus Softener

A callus is a hard, thickened area that builds up on the skin as a result of pressure or friction. Writing as much as I do, I'm constantly plagued with calluses forming on my finger. Feet are also frequently subject to callus formation due to shoes that do not fit properly.

Annoying calluses are made by the building up of epidermis, the tough, hard outer layer of the skin. But they can be easily removed. Here's how to do it at low cost.

You'll need 1/2 cup castor oil, 1/2 cup paraffin wax, 1 tablespoon white soap chips or powder, and 1 teaspoon sodium thiosulfate. Put the oil, wax, and soap in the top section of a double boiler and heat until blended. Cool down to about 100°F. and stir in the sodium thiosulfate. Store in impervious plastic or glass jars. To use, apply to callus before bedtime (the consistency will be like a heavy grease) and wrap with gauze to protect bed clothing. Wash off with hot water in the morning. Repeat as necessary.

Cuticle Remover

Our hands are one of the most important parts of the human anatomy. And they are also prominent to the observation of others. When we eat with others, attend business meetings, point out things or shake hands they're out front for all to see. So, good hand grooming is essential to making a favorable impression on those around us, and fingernails are a most important factor. Well-shaped, clean nails are of course essential, but there is something else, the cuticle.

Cuticle is dead skin that may be found protruding over the nail at its base. When softened it is easy to remove. This formula will provide you with a good softener. You'll need 1 tablespoon trisodium phosphate (TSP), 3 tablespoons glycerin, and water to suit. Stir the TSP into the glycerin mixing thoroughly, and add sufficient water to form a brushable paste. Apply to base of fingernails and allow to soak in. Remove with soap and water using a fingernail brush. Store in glass or impervious plastic container. (Caution: TSP is a skin irritant. Use rubber gloves in the preparation of this formula.)

Dandruff Treatment

Dandruff is a condition of the scalp which is covered by flakes of skin that are produced by excessive secretion of the sebaceous glands. This condition is also accompanied by an increase in bacteria and fungi which may add to the problem.

The real cause of dandruff is not known and it's probably not a serious condition. However, scalp itching and irritation frequently occur in the more severe cases. But many folks who have dandruff feel that the real problem is a cosmetic one. When wearing dark clothes, dandruff makes you look as if you've been in a snowstorm.

No permanent cure for dandruff is yet known. However, use of this formula together with frequent shampooing usually results in control. Any skin condition that is severe should be seen by a dermatologist, of course.

You'll need 1 tablespoon salicylic acid, 3 tablespoons glycerin, and 1 quart of isopropyl alcohol. Mix the salicylic acid and glycerin into the alcohol, stir well, and transfer to glass or impervious plastic bottles. To use, dab this mixture on the scalp with a tuft of cotton at bedtime, and shampoo hair the next morning. You may want to cover your pillow with a towel before going to bed. (Caution: Isopropyl alcohol is moderately toxic and flammable.)

Disinfectant for Shoes

Perspiration is a liquid given off by the skin. While it consists chiefly of water it also contains salt, phosphorus, sulphur, and small amounts of waste matter. Perspiring is a continuous process even though its physical presence can't always be seen. In the presence of heat or exertion, however, the moisture becomes visible on the skin.

Most unexposed parts of the body are covered with porous clothing that permits air contact with the skin. The notable exception is our feet. Each of these marvels of engineering is usually encased in a housing of relatively impervious leather, which excludes the air from contacting the skin. And, as a result, the unevaporated perspiration permeates the lining of the shoes, where bacterial action causes deterioration. But here's a way to overcome this problem inexpensively and simply.

You'll need 1 tablespoon of formaldehyde, which you can get from a druggist, and 1/4 cup water. Mix the formaldehyde into the water and store in a glass or impervious plastic container. To use, swab the shoe linings using a cotton swab and allow to dry before wearing. Repeat as often as necessary. (Caution: Formaldehyde is toxic by inhalation, skin contact, and ingestion. Do not wear shoes until solution has dried and therefore evaporated. Handle carefully, using rubber gloves.)

Dry Hand Cleaner

The scene is the service entrance to an auto repair station. You've decided that a new car is just too expensive, but the old buggy isn't running up to par, so what to do? Maybe a "tune up" is the answer, which brought you to the service island. Sooner or later a "service consultant" (that's what it says he is on his white coat) will greet you and diagnose the problem. The estimate? $135.00. But of course that's only an estimate. The actual cost could be much more, but seldom less. You've been there before, paid high prices and had to return again to repay for what should have been done right the first time, so you decide there must be a better way. And for many people there is. Do it yourself.

Many fine books are available that give step-by-step instructions on how to do your own auto maintenance, and a lot of people are doing just that. But when you do, your hands and arms will get dirty, which brings me to the point — a good cleaner that you can make simply and inexpensively to remove the grime and dirt from your hands and arms.

You'll need 1 cup soap powder, 1 cup fine sawdust, and 1 tablespoon borax. Dry mix these ingredients together and store in a glass, metal, or impervious plastic container. To use, wet skin area to be cleaned and rub about a teaspoon of the cleaner on skin. Rinse with clear water.

Earwax Softener

The ear is generally regarded as the second most important sense organ in the human body next to the eye. It consists of three main parts: the outer, middle, and inner. The outer ear catches the sounds and transmits them to the middle ear. Here, the sound waves become vibrations that channel to the inner portion where nerve impulses are formed and sent to the brain. A secondary function of the inner ear is to provide equilibrium.

Earwax is formed by glands in the tissue directly under the skin and injected into the ear canal. The purpose of both the wax and the hairs is to act as a barrier against the entrance of foreign matter. This wax can build up to an excessive level to the point where it can impair hearing or, in extreme cases, even cause temporary deafness. If the wax is softened, the excess will usually discharge itself. But if it does not do so by itself your doctor should be consulted, of course. In editing this recipe, my good wife who is a registered nurse, recalled that in her early days of training she learned: "never put anything in your ear that's smaller than your elbow." I'm sure any medical doctor would agree. Here's an inexpensive, easy to make formula that keeps earwax from becoming hard.

You'll need 1/8 teaspoon of bicarbonate of soda (measure this by using a 1/4 measuring teaspoon and estimating 1/2 of it), 1/4 cup glycerin (U.S.P. grade), and 1/2 cup distilled water, (or tap water that has been boiled for at least 3 minutes and allowed to cool to room temperature). Mix the glycerin into the water and stir. Then add the bicarbonate of soda. Store in sterilized dropper bottles. (Note: For smaller quantity reduce ingredients in proportion.) To use, put several drops in ear at bedtime.

Effervescent Bath Salts

Few things are more relaxing than a hot bath. But even this can be improved upon by the addition of a compound that causes bubbles to form. Their action as they rise to the water's surface has an almost massage-like effect on the skin.

Each bubble is literally a tiny envelope of water surrounding a harmless nontoxic gas. As we all know, gases rise to the surface because they are lighter in weight than water. For those of you readers who do not already know, it may be interesting to learn just how these gas bubbles are formed. The principle involved here is that of a base (bicarbonate of soda) neutralizing an acid (tartaric). When these chemicals are mixed together nothing happens. However, when water is added the base neutralizes the acid causing a reaction which forms the gas.

Personal

To make effervescent bath salts you'll need 9 tablespoons of bicarbonate of soda, 7 1/2 tablespoons of tartaric acid (cream of tartar), and 2 tablespoons cornstarch. Simply dry mix these three ingredients thoroughly and add a few drops of any water-soluble perfume if desired. Use about 2 tablespoons to a tub of water, or your preference. Store in airtight glass, metal, or impervious plastic containers.

Eyelash and Eyebrow Conditioner

The human eye is similar to a T.V. camera. It receives light from the outside and focuses it on a delicate screen inside to form an image which is converted to electrical impulses that are sent to the brain via the optic nerve where the image is seen.

Unlike the T.V. camera however, the human eye has a far more delicate lens that needs to be protected against the entrance of foreign matter such as dust and dirt. Nature has provided us with built in safeguards — the eyelids, eyelashes, and eyebrows.

The eye is the most important sensory organ of the human body and deserves all the protection it can be given. Management of industrial manufacturing firms recognize this and have a rigid rule that all employees and visitors must wear safety glasses in areas where eyes may be harmed.

Here's a formula that will improve the appearance of eyelashes and eyebrows as well as make them a more effective barrier against foreign materials. All containers and mixing utensils for this formula should be sterilized or at least thoroughly washed. You'll need 1/4 cup petroleum jelly, 1/4 cup castor oil, and 1/4 teaspoon paraffin wax. Put all three ingredients together in the top of a double boiler (never over direct heat) and heat until melted. Cool down to just above solidification point and pour into glass or impervious plastic jars. To use, apply sparingly to eyebrows and lashes with soft brush.

The Formula Book 2

Face Lotion

A clean clear complexion is an asset to anyone. But unfortunately our poor faces take such a beating from dozens of contaminants that we all need to give our skin special care.

As our air becomes more polluted our skin takes abuse. Oxides of nitrogen, sulfuric acid, and particulate matter, such as the black smoke we see from diesel trucks, trains, and poorly maintained automobile engines all contribute to pollution as do dust and dirt. Dermatologists whom I have queried agree that as pollution increases, they are seeing more and more evidence of skin disorders. And the best preventive measure appears to be keeping the pores clean and free of contaminants.

Here's a formula that's easy and inexpensive to make and seems to do a good job. You'll need 1/4 cup glycerin, 1 3/4 cups isopropyl alcohol, 3 cups water, and a few drops of water soluble perfume, if desired. Mix the first three ingredients together while stirring. Add perfume if desired. Isopropyl alcohol has a mild, pleasant odor which may partially mask the perfume. However, as it evaporates from the skin the odor disappears leaving the perfume scent intact. To use, wash face thoroughly and then splash on face lotion. Store excess in a glass or impervious plastic container.

Face Powder

Having been raised in a family with two older sisters, and now having a family that consists of one wife, four daughters and two granddaughters, I feel that I qualify as being "female oriented." And it's been a rich experience to say the least. The statement "never underestimate the power of a woman" is a gross understatement. Fellow men, let's face it. We don't have a chance. But I for one wouldn't have it any other way.

Over the years (before *The Formula* column and *The Formula Book*) I've seen many pounds and gallons of cos-

Personal

metics used. And what I paid for would amount to a staggering sum. Ah, what price beauty! Of course in the more recent years we have made our own. Having been an observer to this "parade of beauty" I've noticed that face powder is a major part of the arsenal of beauty aids, and it's expensive to buy. So here's a formula you can make up yourself and save a lot of expense.

You'll need 4 cups of talc, 1/8 cup boric acid, 1 cup cornstarch, oil soluble dye, and oil soluble perfume to suit. Mix the dry ingredients thoroughly and then mix in the dye and perfume. (Note: A flour sifter is excellent for mixing, blending, and removing any foreign particles.) Store in glass, impervious plastic, or paperboard containers.

Facial Bleach

It's ironic that some people will go to great expense to travel to the lands of sunshine to tan their skin, while others prefer to bleach it. But of all the great things about this country we live in, one of the greatest is that we have our choice as to what we want to do.

Human skin is actually an organ of the body, and the largest one at that. It serves many functions in that it is a protective envelope, and largely serves as a thermostat to control body temperature by the process of evaporation.

If your inclination is toward lighter colored skin, here's a formula for a bleach that will accomplish it.

All containers and mixing utensils should be sterilized or at least thoroughly washed. You'll need 1 1/2 tablespoons sodium perborate, and 2 cups calcium carbonate. Dry mix these powders together. To use, make a paste with water and apply with a soft brush. Leave on overnight and remove in the morning with clear water. Bleaching effect is temporary; repeat as needed. Some people do have allergies. It is therefore suggested that a small amount be applied at first to determine if an allergic reaction takes place. If it does, use should be discontinued. Store in glass or impervious plastic container.

The Formula Book 2

Facial Pore Closer

Skin performs many functions for us. It acts as a waterproof covering for the body, transmits signals to the brain, excretes wastes, and aids in the control of body temperature. Where I live, in toasty Tucson, the humidity is low and 100°F. plus temperatures are common in the summer months. Getting out of a swimming pool is quite an experience in that your skin becomes ice cold. This is caused by the rapid evaporation of water on the skin, and works on the same principle as a mechanical refrigeration unit.

The skin contains sebaceous glands that secrete the oil which collects in the pores. Now add dust and dirt, which we are all exposed to, and the plugged pores result in blackheads and skin infections. But these problems can be reduced by treating the pores with an astringent to reduce the possibility of their being collectors of dirt. Here's the way to do it.

All containers and mixing utensils should be sterilized or at least thoroughly washed. You'll need 1 tablespoon powdered alum, 1 cup talc, 1 tablespoon boric acid, 1/2 cup isopropyl alcohol, and 1 cup water. Mix the isopropyl alcohol with the water, and add the alum, talc, and boric acid to the solution. To use, wash face thoroughly to remove accumulated dirt and oil. Before bedtime apply facial pore closer liberally with cotton. Rinse with clear water in the morning. Store in glass or impervious plastic container. (Caution: Isopropyl alcohol is toxic and flammable.)

Finger Stain Remover

Fingers are one of the more important parts of our anatomy. When you stop to think about it, we do take them pretty much for granted.

Several years ago my wife Eileen underwent delicate surgery on her right hand. Her doctor, who is regarded as one of the top hand surgeons, explained the physiology of the hand to us. What a marvel of engineering that is.

Considering the use and abuse, it's inevitable that fingers become stained at times and this is especially true for folks who smoke. So if you too have this problem, here's an easy formula that can help.

You'll need 2 tablespoons sodium sulfate (a photo shop will have this) and 1/2 cup water. Mix the two ingredients together. To use: Apply to stain with cotton and allow to stand for about 15 minutes. Remove with soap and water. Some people do have allergies. It is therefore suggested that a small amount be applied at first to determine if an allergic reaction takes place. If it does, use should be discontinued. Store in glass or impervious plastic container.

Foot Powder

Feet are essential to our mobility. But what do we do to take care of them? Practically nothing. The average American's automobile gets better care.

When you stop to think about it, feet, with a relatively small surface area, support an entire heavy body. Surely they deserve more consideration than they are given. Well-fitting footwear plus the services of a podiatrist, if problems such as ingrown toenails or bunions appear, are essential.

The excessive moisture buildup in our footwear results in an ideal place for bacteria and fungi to grow and reproduce. And to compound the problem, many of us wear socks made of synthetic materials that repel, rather than absorb moisture.

But here's a formula that will help to keep your feet dry and comfortable. All you need to make it is 1 3/4 cups cornstarch, and 1/4 cup boric acid. Dry mix these two materials together. To use, sprinkle on feet before putting on socks. Store excess powder in a glass or impervious plastic container.

The Formula Book 2

Lanolin Hand and Face Lotion

Sheep, those gentle creatures that are seen by the thousands grazing on our western plains, provide us with many of the good things in life. How about a rack of lamb? Or lamb chops? Or mutton chops such as the ones served by Keen's English Chop House in New York where Daniel Webster's clay pipe hangs on the ceiling among their collection? Or wool? And there's another valuable material they provide us with — wool fat, also known as lanolin.

By and large, the wool we use for clothing and other fabrics has the lanolin removed from it, which makes lanolin available for other uses such as in this formula. There is a notable exception, however. Our Canadian friends do not remove the lanolin from some wool that is used to knit the heavy sweaters almost everyone wears in that beautiful cold country. By leaving the fat in the wool, a high degree of water repellency results, serving as protection against rain and snow. Here's a formula for a hand and face cream that contains lanolin as an important ingredient.

All containers and mixing utensils should be sterilized or at least thoroughly washed. You'll need 1/2 teaspoon powdered soap, 2 tablespoons distilled water, 2 tablespoons lanolin, and 2 tablespoons glycerin. Mix the soap and glycerin into the water. Now add the lanolin with constant, rapid stirring. Water-soluble perfume may be added as desired. Use as you would any face or hand cream. Store in glass, metal, or impervious plastic container.

Leather Cleaner

The broadest, and perhaps too simplistic, definition of leather is that it's the skin of an animal, fish, or reptile that has been treated chemically by a process known as tanning to preserve it.

Personal

Making leather is an ancient art that the Egyptians practiced thousands of years ago, using oak bark in the tanning process. In Europe, guilds of leather makers were formed, which are believed to have been the forerunners of labor unions.

Leather is a porous material that breathes. This fact sets it apart from synthetics that generally do not. While plastics have become a satisfactory substitute for a number of natural materials such as in textiles, for example, they have not been as successful in replacing leather in certain applications such as shoes and gloves, where a material's ability to "breathe" is an advantage. But if the pores of leather are permitted to become clogged with foreign materials such as dirt, the ability to breathe and be flexible is impaired. This formula will do a good job of keeping your leather objects clean and flexible.

All you will need is 3/4 cup isopropyl alcohol, 1/2 cup white distilled vinegar, and 1 1/2 cups water. Mix these three ingredients together and stir. Store in glass or impervious plastic containers. To use, dampen cloth or sponge with the mixture and rub into leather until clean. (Caution: Isopropyl alcohol is toxic and flammable.)

Liquid Underarm Deodorant

The American obsession with smelling good is a commendable one, but the cost of being socially acceptable for a family of four is unacceptable. When you see how little it costs to make a quality deodorant right in your own kitchen, you'll be shocked at the prices you have been paying for fancy packaging and outlandishly expensive advertising. Here's an inflation-beater formula for a highly effective deodorant.

You'll need some powdered alum and a plastic spray bottle, as well as water soluble perfume if you desire a scented product. (Alum is an astringent that helps close your pores to prevent excessive perspiration.)

Mix 2 tablespoons of alum into 1 pint of warm water. Add a small amount of cologne or shaving lotion for scent. Transfer to a spray bottle, or apply with a dab of cotton or soft cloth.

Oxygen Foot Bath

It has been said that bread is the staff of life. But this is not entirely true. I vote for oxygen. Without it wheat couldn't grow to make the bread, and we wouldn't be around to eat it. In short, oxygen is absolutely essential to life. Oxygen was discovered by Priestley in 1774, and is the most abundant element in the world, forming about one-fifth of the air we breathe at sea level.

Here's a formula that releases oxygen to soothe tired feet. Try it and I think you'll find it beneficial, as I have.

You'll need 1 tablespoon sodium thiosulfate, 1 tablespoon sodium perborate, 6 tablespoons sodium borate, and 3/4 cup sodium bicarbonate. Dry mix these ingredients together and store in impervious plastic or glass containers. To use, mix 2 tablespoons in 2 quarts of warm water for a foot bath. The released bubbling action makes for a soothing and relaxing experience.

Protective Hand Cream

Hands are one of the most important parts of the human anatomy. Before writing this recipe, I tried an experiment which demonstrated just how much I take my hands for granted. You might want to try it too. I had my left hand tied to my belt so that it was not usable and went on about my work. What a handicap. No longer do I take them for granted.

Hands take a lot of abuse. We subject them to all kinds of indignities every day, and then many people spend a lot of money on a myriad of potions in an attempt to restore them to their normal condition. It is said that an ounce of prevention is worth a pound of cure. So why not protect your hands before you expose them.

Personal

Here's a simple inexpensive formula for a cream that works well. You'll need 1 tablespoon gelatin, 3/4 cup glycerin and 1 1/2 cups water. Stir the glycerin into the water. Heat in top of a double boiler and add the gelatin. Cool and store in glass or impervious plastic jars. To use, rub into hands thoroughly before exposure.

Rubbing Alcohol Compound

There are two types of alcohol that can be used for making this compound: (1) isopropyl, or (2) denatured. Denatured alcohol is ethyl alcohol that has been intentionally adulterated to make it unfit for human consumption. Many different chemicals are used as additives depending on the end use of the alcohol. For example, alcohol that is to be used as an industrial solvent would be far more drastically denatured than alcohol that is to be used as a rubbing compound. But remember, all denatured alcohols must not be taken internally as they are toxic to varying degrees. They are also flammable, of course.

Isopropyl alcohol is my choice for a number of reasons. (1) It is readily available in small quantities; (2) it is lower in cost; and (3) although it is toxic it is far less so than most of the denatured alcohols. But it is also flammable and should be used with the proper precautions.

To make up this formula you will need 1 3/4 cups of either denatured or isopropyl alcohol, 1/4 cup glycerin, and 1/2 cup water. Mix these three ingredients together, store in glass or impervious plastic bottles and keep container tightly sealed to minimize loss by evaporation. (Caution: Both denatured and isopropyl alcohol are toxic by ingestion and flammable.)

Tar and Nicotine Stain Remover for Hands

Tobacco is an annual plant belonging to the nightshade family. At the top of a mature tobacco plant will be found a cluster of pink or yellow blossoms. The seeds are tiny and black and 1/2 ounce will produce enough plants for an acre of ground.

The two components that we are concerned with for this formula are: nicotine and tar. Nicotine is a white substance which is highly poisonous in its pure form. Many useful chemicals are derived from it, the alkaloid that gives tobacco its narcotic effect. Of importance to this formula is the fact that, while in its pure form nicotine is colorless, exposure to air causes it to change to a brown color. This, together with the brown tar, frequently causes unsightly finger stains, especially among cigarette smokers. If you have a problem with finger stains, here's a formula that will remove them.

You'll need 1 tablespoon of beeswax, 1/2 tablespoon paraffin wax, 5 tablespoons of mineral oil, 1 tablespoon powdered pumice, 1/2 tablespoon borax, and 3 tablespoons water. Melt the beeswax, paraffin wax and mineral oil in top section of double boiler. Turn off heat and add pumice and borax with constant stirring. Continue stirring and add water. To use, rub into stained skin area and wash with soap and water. Store in impervious plastic, glass, or metal jars.

Toilette Water

Perfume goes back for centuries and has been widely used since then. While there are many kinds of perfumes, including synthetics made in the laboratory, the most common are those derived from plants. In some plants, the fragrant oils, known as essential oil, are present in the leaves while in others they are present in the flowers.

The essential oils are extracted by means of steam distillation whereby the flowers or leaves are boiled with water and the steam is condensed back into liquid form. This condensate is then redistilled to separate the oil and water; however, some of the oil does remain with the water, which then becomes known as rose water, lavender water, etc. These are the fragrances called for in the following formula.

Personal

You'll need 5 tablespoons isopropyl alcohol, 5 tablespoons glycerin, 2 tablespoons borax and 2 pints water, and fragrance water to suit. Mix all ingredients together stirring as each one is put in. Store in capped glass or impervious plastic bottles. Isopropyl alcohol has a slight pleasant odor which will partially mask the floral scent. However, it will evaporate from the skin so the scent you put in will be present on the skin. (Caution: Isopropyl alcohol must never be taken internally and is, of course, flammable.)

Underarm Deodorant Pads

A soft flannel disc used to clean a shotgun barrel is also ideal to use as a pad for applying underarm deodorant. I feel that whenever it's possible to use an existing material that is mass produced, there are definite cost advantages.

Round discs of flannel cloth are produced by the billions for gun cleaning. These same discs are just about the right size for underarm deodorant pads. They're available at any sporting goods store at a nominal cost.

To make up a formula for underarm deodorant pads, you'll need 3 tablespoons of powdered alum and 1 pint water. Dissolve the alum in the water. Place the flannel discs in a glass or impervious plastic jar and pour the solution over them, until thoroughly saturated. To use, rub a pad on area to be protected.

Winter Hand Protective Lotion

When the skin on your hands looks like ice skaters' tracks on a pond and when your hands feel as if the blades of the ice skates have been cutting into them, a fancily packaged "store-bought" lotion will probably leave you smelling like a bouquet of flowers — but no better protected than when you make your own.

The Formula Book 2

Make up this simple mixture to use *before* exposure to the elements for real protection. Rub it on your hands again after you've worked outside for added effectiveness.

You'll need gelatin (the unflavored kind from the grocery store) and glycerin.

Heat 1 envelope of gelatin and 3/4 cup of glycerin in the top of a double boiler. Add 1 1/2 cups of water slowly, pouring in a constant stream while stirring the mixture. Water soluble perfume such as cologne may be added if desired. Apply sparingly to skin before exposure to winter weather. Store in glass or impervious plastic container.

NOTES

Name of Formula: _____

Date Made: _____

Ingredients and amounts: _____

_____

_____

_____

Label: Ingredients and caution warnings

Observations: _____

_____

_____

_____

_____

- - - - - - - - - -

Name of Formula: _____

Date Made: _____

Ingredients and amounts: _____

_____

_____

_____

Label: Ingredients and caution warnings

Observations: ___ _____

_____

_____

_____

_____

NOTES

Name of Formula: _____

Date Made: _____

Ingredients and amounts: _____

_____

_____

_____

Label: Ingredients and caution warnings

Observations: _____

_____

_____

_____

_____

- - - - - - - - - -

Name of Formula: _____

Date Made: _____

Ingredients and amounts: _____

_____

_____

_____

Label: Ingredients and caution warnings

Observations: _____

_____

_____

_____

_____

3
Automotive and Mechanical

Automotive and Mechanical

Auto Fuel Ice Preventative

Ole man winter has arrived!! Here is a way to avoid a frustrating situation — the frozen fuel line.

If you have ever been caught in this situation you'll be glad to hear of this easy, economical way to go through winter without this problem.

All you need for protection against frozen fuel lines are these inexpensive ingredients which can be purchased from your local drug and hardware store.

Mix together 1 quart of isopropyl alcohol (91%) (from the drugstore) with 1 teaspoon of light lubricating oil and 1 teaspoon of pine oil (both available at the hardware store). Use 1/2 cup for each 10 gallons of gasoline during the winter months. Make it a habit to use this additive each time you fill your tank. Store in glass or impervious plastic bottle. (Caution: Isopropyl alcohol is flammable and toxic. Handle with care.)

Automobile and Boat Top Dressing

In my opinion the lines of a convertible are beautiful. And what a great feeling to put down the top on that first warm spring day and absorb the sunshine. And then when you get to the lake and launch your boat, getting even more exposure to old Sol.

On occasion I allow myself the luxury of reminiscing about my youth. I had a 1933 used Ford convertible that was beautiful. It was a tan color with a light beige top. When I think about it now I realize that it would do anything that a new model does today and some things a lot better at about 1/10th the cost. So where's the progress? But those canvas or fabric tops, whether on a boat or a car, do need attention. Here's how you can keep them waterproofed, and dirt resistant.

You'll need 1 quart of isopropyl alcohol, 1/8 cup white shellac, and 1 teaspoon castor oil. Mix all three ingredients together and store in metal, glass, or impervious plastic container. To use: Wash material with soap and water to remove existing dirt and allow to dry thoroughly. Paint on a thin coat of the solution with a soft brush and be sure surface is completely dry before lowering top. Store in glass, metal or impervious plastic container. (Caution: Isopropyl alcohol is toxic and both it and the shellac are flammable.)

Auto Windshield Cleaner

In the interest of safety and eye care, automobile windshields and windows should be kept clean at all times. Folks who wash their own cars spend as much as 100 hours per year doing this job. So any shortcuts in time are worthwhile indeed. When you take both the inner and outer surfaces of windows and windshields into consideration, and then add mirrors and light lenses, you find that glass surfaces are a major part of the total area you need to clean.

Because of the exorbitant price of gas and oil products many of us patronize the self-service stations. The savings are substantial, but if we want clean glass we must again do it ourselves between the weekly general car washing. Here's an easy way to make an inexpensive formula that takes a lot of the hard work out of glass cleaning.

You'll need 1/2 cup calcium carbonate (chalk), 1/4 cup bicarbonate of soda, 1 cup diatomaceous earth (fuller's earth), and 1 cup water. Mix the three powders together and add the water, slowly with stirring, to make a paste. To use: Apply to glass with a cloth pad or sponge, and polish with a dry lint-free cloth. Store in glass, metal, or impervious plastic container.

Auto Windshield Insect Remover

In the days before the automobile, the surrey, pulled by a team of "high-stepping strutters," was a common sight. My father used to tell me that a rig like this was

Automotive and Mechanical

just as much a prized possession as an automobile is to some people today. And the better rigs had windshields, just as cars now have.

Insects and bugs were around then just as they are now, but the snail's pace of the rig compared with the modern car's speed gave the bugs a chance to get out of the way. I'm sure the bugs don't mean to mess us up the way they do but, after all, what chance do they have against that "Belchfire Eight" gas guzzler charging down the road at them like a streak of lightning?

This formula is intended to be used in the windshield washer container under the hood. All you need is 2 quarts of isopropyl alcohol and 2 quarts of water. While it serves no practical purpose, you can put in a few drops of blue food coloring if you want to make it look like the high-priced product. Mix the ingredients together and transfer to your windshield washer tank. Store excess in glass or impervious plastic bottle. (Caution: Isopropyl alcohol is toxic by ingestion and flammable.)

Gasoline Vapor Lock Compound

There are many different types of pumps. Some move liquids while others move semisolids and gases. But each type is designed for its specific job. So when a pump is made to transport a liquid, and the liquid suddenly changes to a vapor (gas), the pump no longer can handle the job that it was made to do.

The fuel pump in your automobile was designed to transport gasoline from the gas tank to the carburetor in its liquid form. But on a hot summer day, the temperature in the pump may turn the liquid gasoline to a vapor (gas) which it was not designed to transport. The result is what's known as vapor lock, which causes the engine to quit for lack of fuel. So you may find yourself sitting in the lane of a busy freeway, sort of like a rock in a fast running stream. To correct this situation temporarily, you can pour cold water over the outer casing of the fuel pump. This will condense the vapors back to a liquid so

The Formula Book 2

it can again be pumped to the carburetor and get you started. For a permanent solution, however, vapor lock needs to be prevented rather than corrected. Here's a formula that will do that.

For this formula you'll need 3/4 cup kerosene and 1/4 cup turpentine. Mix these two ingredients together with stirring. To use, add 2 tablespoons to each gallon of gasoline in extremely hot weather. (Caution: Both kerosene and turpentine are flammable and toxic by ingestion as well. Handle with due precautions. Store in glass or metal container.)

4

Garden and Agricultural

Garden and Agricultural

Acidifying or Alkalizing Potted Plant Soil

My wife and partner Eileen, has an amazing way with plants and children. Her method, as far as I've been able to understand it, is to be firm while being fair and just. This philosophy of hers has resulted in four lovely daughters, all of whom have done well, and a jungle of house plants that threaten to "take over" our living area.

I know it may seem far-fetched to some of you readers, as it once was to me, but she does have a rapport with her plants. Her formula seems to be, "I'll treat you right, and then I expect you to treat me right." And they do. Her two most important elements, as far as both children and plants are concerned, are love and a good diet.

But there's another factor that's important. Some plants prefer an acid soil and some an alkaline. So here are two formulas that will increase or decrease the alkalinity or acidity of the soil.

If you need to increase the acid in the soil, 4 tablespoons of powdered alum in a quart of water will do it. Or, if you want to increase the alkalinity, the same amount of bicarbonate of soda will accomplish it. Store in glass, metal, or impervious plastic container.

Ant Repellent

Have you ever wondered, as I have, what possible good can come from pests that seem to serve no purpose other than to annoy us? I've never known what possible reason God had for putting them on our planet earth. The common rat is a good example. Why are they here? What good do they do? None that I know of. They contaminate and destroy causing billions of dollars of damage each year. But I also wonder this. If by a magic formula all rats could be destroyed, would we then discover the reason for their being put here in the first place? Your guess is as good as mine.

But to the subject of ants. I'm not smart enough to know why they're here, but I prefer not to have them devour my garden, so here's a formula that I use to repel them and send them on their way.

You'll need 2 tablespoons of sassafras leaves and 2 cups water. Boil the leaves in the water for 5 minutes, cool and strain. Paint the liquid in ant runways. It will send them on their way. Store liquid in glass or impervious plastic containers.

Caterpillar Tree Bands

Moths and butterflies are amazing insects found in all parts of the world. Of more than one hundred thousand identified species, approximately ten thousand are native to the United States. Wing spans range from over a foot in the Indian Atlas Moth to the minute span of the Gilded Moth — less than the diameter of the head of a pin.

The breathtaking beauty of many moths and butterflies results from white, black, red, and yellow pigments in the scales found on the wings. Overlapping scales which work as prisms to break up light rays account for the blues, greens and iridescent metallic shades. But don't be lulled into false security by all this beauty. While moths and butterflies are harmless to your garden, sex comes along and "rears its ugly head." Then they lay eggs and all h--- breaks loose. From the eggs, larvae, such as caterpillars, hatch with a full blown appetite for tender green things such as tiny new leaves on trees and shrubs. So if you're looking forward to shade from big leaves in the summer, it's wise to protect the little ones in the spring. This can be easily and inexpensively done by painting caterpillar tree bands around the trunks. You can make them yourself. Here's how you do it.

You'll need 1 1/2 cups powdered rosin (you can get this from an athletic supply store), 1 cup linseed oil, and 1 tablespoon of ordinary paraffin canning wax. Put all three ingredients together in the top of a double boiler (never over direct heat), heat and stir until melted and

Garden and Agricultural

mixed. When cooled, transfer to a metal, impervious plastic, or glass container. To use, paint a band about 3" wide around the trunk of the tree to be protected.

Chemical Flower Garden

Crystallography is one of the most interesting facets of science. Crystals, from those found in caves that probably took thousands of years "to grow," to those found in rock candy that can be produced in a matter of a few minutes, have one thing in common; the atoms and molecules are always arranged in a regular three-dimensional pattern. Conversely, a solid that has no crystalline structure is called amorphous. A good example of this is in the petroleum waxes. Paraffin has a definite crystalline structure while amorphous wax has none. But combined they form a useful product for many applications.

Unlike our other formulas, this one does not result in a product you can use. However, the fun of seeing crystals grow, and the decorative effect, seem to me to justify its inclusion.

You'll need a porous brick, a shallow pan or bowl, 12 tablespoons salt, 12 tablespoons water, 12 tablespoons of laundry bluing, 2 tablespoons of household ammonia, and 8 drops of red, blue, or green ink. Mix the salt, water, laundry bluing and household ammonia in a suitable container. Place brick in pan or bowl and fill with solution to 2" on side of brick. Add your choice of colored ink in spots on the top surface of brick. Capillary action will cause solution to migrate to top surface where colored crystals will grow.

Compost Making

Mother Nature has provided us with a closed system that is ecologically nearly perfect. A good example of this is the tree. The root system supplies water and nutrients, and when fall comes the leaves enhance the further growth of the tree during the next growing season. Unfortunately, man, having no real appreciation for this marvelous system, has come along and largely destroyed it. Instead of leaving it as nature intended, we rake up the leaves and burn them, polluting the atmosphere. But there is a way we can follow nature's plan and reap the rewards of lush growth and increased crop yields. That way is making and using compost. And, it's free.

Compost is partially decomposed organic material that can be returned to the earth to improve the productivity of the soil. It increases water-holding capacity and improves soil structure and drainage, which aids in the removal of harmful salts. The process of making compost utilizes organic waste materials, giving them a positive value. Any organic material such as newspapers, paper boxes and bags, wood shavings and sawdust, leaves, grass clippings and kitchen wastes can be used. But there are materials that can't be composted. Examples of these are glass, metal, plastics, crockery, bones and wax-coated paper.

The process of composting is to provide the preferred bacteria with conditions ideally suited to permit them to reduce the mass to an odorless substance by decomposition. Air, and the correct amount of moisture are the two most essential elements. For this reason, the compost pile should be built on the surface of the ground, and never in a pit. Following are the procedures for successful composting.

Step 1: Contain the area where your compost pile will be with a fence that permits the circulation of air and keeps the material from blowing away or being scattered by animals or birds. The fencing can be chicken wire, chain link, or snow fencing. Our preference is the snow fencing, as it is inexpensive, flexible so it can be used as a gate, and attractive.

Step 2: Next, make a flat top pile of composting material on the ground inside the fenced area. As previously mentioned, use any organic material such as kitchen wastes, paper, etc. (In our operation, we put

Garden and Agricultural

waste materials in newspapers or paper bags before putting them on the pile, as this eliminates the problem of flies.)

Step 3: After about 12" of composting material has been spread out in the bin, cover the entire surface with about 2" to 3" of garden soil or dehydrated manure, which will provide the bacteria that causes decomposition. Then continue adding composting materials until another 12" has been built up, etc.

Step 4: The amount of moisture you add to your compost pile is very important. The pile should be damp at all times, but never wet. And it should never have an objectionable odor. But if it does, it will be because of too much moisture. This will be your sign to back off on the amount of water.

Step 5: Composting can and should be a continuous process. So it is advisable to make your fencing cover an area sufficient in size to provide two bins, with a divider of snow fence between them. After your first pile has been allowed to build up, heat, and decompose for about six weeks, it should be forked to the second bin. Thus, the top layer of the first bin will become the bottom of the second bin. Now you can start to use the top layer of the second bin while a new supply is being built up in the first bin.

Step 6: Relatively large amounts of compost are needed to improve soil and it should be applied frequently, preferably before planting time. The method we find works best is to spread up to 6" of compost over the area, and work into the soil.

Composting is a rewarding effort. Actually it's like getting something for nothing, in that wastes are converted to a usable product.

Garden Insecticide — All Purpose

With a world food shortage being predicted by agricultural experts, home gardening may become a necessity rather than a hobby. A small 400-square-foot plot, properly managed, can supply all the vegetables needed by a family of four. And it's fun and rewarding.

Dr. Walt Menninger, world-renowned psychiatrist, in his nationally syndicated column, "In-Sights," talks about *The Formula Book* and I quote: "Some people might justify buying this book on the basis of saving money and coping with inflation. I suspect an equally powerful motive is satisfying the psychological drive toward mastery and self-sufficiency." And I know from personal experience that several hours in my garden erases business worries and brings relaxation.

When you have a garden, you can be sure of having an insect problem that must be dealt with. The Environmental Protection Agency (EPA) has banned many of the insecticides that have been widely used, such as chlordane, D.D.T. etc. So it's necessary to get down to some old proven basic ones. And this garden insecticide — all purpose — qualifies. Here's the formula.

You'll need 1 cup pyrethrum flowers and 1 gallon of ordinary fuel oil. Mix the two and stir thoroughly. Allow to stand 48 hours and strain. Store in glass, impervious plastic, or metal containers. Spray leaves of plants to be protected but be cautious; the fuel oil could harm some delicate plants, so treat only one leaf as a test before spraying entire foliage.

Hydroponic Plant Food

While my feeling is that the best fruits and vegetables are grown by conventional methods, i.e., in soil rich in organic humus and natural fertilizer such as manure, there is an alternative method which should be offered as an option. This is hydroponic feeding.

In hydroponic growing, soil is replaced by a medium such as gravel or sand. Whereas the function of soil is to feed the plant, gravel serves only as a medium to hold it in place. Nutrients are then fed to the bed in liquid form where they are absorbed by the plant. This is a basic description of hydroponic feeding; however, there

Garden and Agricultural

are other modifications and combinations that are used. Here is a basic formula for a hydroponic solution.

You will need 3 tablespoons of potassium nitrate, 2 tablespoons of calcium sulfate, 2 tablespoons of magnesium sulfate, 1 tablespoon of monocalcium phosphate, 1 teaspoon ammonium sulfate, and 10 gallons of water. Mix all dry ingredients together and dissolve in the water. Note: These are all agricultural chemicals that are available in most garden shops. To use, apply liquid to bed as required with sprinkling can or by constant drip. Store in glass or impervious plastic container.

Potted Plant Fertilizer

Talk to a plant? Seemed crazy to me when I first heard about it, but now I'm not so sure. As we all know some people have a "green thumb" while others have poor luck with growing anything. Could this be caused by lack of communication?

We know that both humans and plants have a complex electrical system, which is essential to communications. A good example of this is the radio. Station WXYZ broadcasts 24 hours a day, but if our radio is not tuned to its frequency we don't hear what is being broadcast. Perhaps the "green thumb" people are in communication with plants where others are not. Regardless of the validity of this theory it's certain that a plant, as any other living thing, must have nourishment or it will die. Here's a formula for a good potted plant fertilizer that you can make easily and inexpensively.

The materials required are 1 cup potassium nitrate, 1/3 cup superphosphate, 2 tablespoons ammonium sulfate, 3 tablespoons urea, 1 speck calcium carbonate, and 1/2 cup fine mason sand. Dry mix these ingredients together. To use, add 1 tablespoon to each pot when first set out, and then 1 tablespoon per month as a side dressing. Store in glass, metal, paper, or impervious plastic container.

The Formula Book 2

Rabbit Repellent II

Rabbits are one of the most common of all American game animals. This, coupled with the fact that they are delicious to eat, probably accounts for the fact that more sportsmen hunt rabbits than any other game.

The reproductive capacity of these cute little animals is well known. Breeding begins at about six months of age, and they have litters of from eight to twelve rabbits twice a year. (You engineer readers, get out your calculators and computers and do a little geometric progression. You'll be amazed at the numbers.) Now all this proliferating can't help but create healthy appetites as Mr. McGregor discovered in dealing with Peter, in his cabbage patch. So if you're having the same problem, here's a formula that will send the little freeloaders on their way.

You'll need 2 pounds hydrated lime and 1 pound calcium carbonate (chalk or whiting). Dry mix these together. Store in metal, impervious plastic, glass, or paper containers. To use, sprinkle powder around the base of plants to be protected.

NOTES

Name of Formula: _____

Date Made: _____

Ingredients and amounts: _____

_____

_____

_____

Label: Ingredients and caution warnings

Observations: _____

_____

_____

_____

_____

- - - - - - - - - -

Name of Formula: _____

Date Made: _____

Ingredients and amounts: _____

_____

_____

_____

Label: Ingredients and caution warnings

Observations: __ _____

_____

_____

_____

NOTES

Name of Formula: _____
Date Made: _____
Ingredients and amounts: _____
_____
_____
_____

Label: Ingredients and caution warnings
Observations: _____
_____
_____
_____
_____

- - - - - - - - - -

Name of Formula: _____
Date Made: _____
Ingredients and amounts: _____
_____
_____
_____

Label: Ingredients and caution warnings
Observations: _____
_____
_____
_____
_____

5

For Sports and Camping

For Sports and Camping

Barbecue Flame Extinguisher

The backyard cookout has become a national institution in America. The onset of spring weather sends fathers everywhere to the outdoors wearing cooks' hats, aprons, and probably carrying the "makins." The smell of cooking hamburgers, hot dogs, bratwurst, and (if a second mortgage has been put on the house or car) even steaks, fills the air. But then, only too often, come the flames to incinerate what's being grilled. There's a simple way to eliminate the ensuing inferno.

Most meats contain a goodly amount of fat. In fact, the best steaks are liberally marbled with it. When this fat becomes liquid as the result of the heat, it drips on the coals, catches fire, and shoots the flames up to the food being grilled. Here's a simple, effective, and inexpensive way to minimize this problem.

You'll need one teaspoon of sodium chloride (table salt) one teaspoon sodium bicarbonate (baking soda) and 1 pint (16 fluid ounces) of water. Mix the salt and soda into the water and transfer solution into plastic spray bottle. To use, direct stream at base of flame. You'll find it far more effective than plain water.

Boot Dubbing

Leather boots are one of the most important items of the outdoor person's wardrobe. They keep feet dry, provide support to ankles when walking over rough terrain and protect against hazards such as insect and snake bites. The experienced outdoor person knows that the entire body can't be comfortable if the feet aren't. So if it's necessary to be economical, as it is for most of us, don't cut corners on your footwear. But, like everything else these days, good boots are expensive. However, with good care and occasional resoling they can last for many years.

If improperly treated leather gets wet, it can become stiff and uncomfortable. so it's advisable to keep boots well oiled to prevent this from occurring. Here's a formula for a product that I have used for years.

You'll need 5 tablespoons of neat's-foot oil, 1 tablespoon tallow, and 1 1/2 tablespoons mineral oil. Heat all three ingredients in top section of a double boiler (never over an open flame) until the piece of tallow is melted. Stir to assure a good mix. Transfer to glass, metal, or impervious plastic containers. To use, first clean boots thoroughly and then rub in mixture to penetrate and soften the leather. Note: For more penetration, heat boots in a low temperature oven (about 100°F.) before applying oil, which should also be warmed.

Canvas Fire Retardant

Canvas is a heavy cloth made of unbleached flax or hemp. Its principal use is where strength and durability are required such as in tents. It is interesting to note that the expression "to canvass" means to sift or examine with care, which is derived from the use of canvas as a sifting cloth.

Camping out is a practice that millions of us have embraced in our efforts to get away from the rat race that we are involved in to make a living and take care of our families. And it's fun. Waking up in the morning to a pot of coffee on an open fire with the promise of bacon and eggs and the kids having a ball is a welcome relief to our workaday world. But there is a danger which should be guarded against.

Untreated canvas, such as a tent or a barrier under a sleeping bag, is a fire hazard. Sparks from a campfire, or the careless use of smoking materials could cause a disaster. This formula will minimize that risk.

You'll need 1/2 cup ammonium phosphate, 1 cup ammonium chloride, and 1 quart of water. Mix these three ingredients together and store in a glass or impervious plastic container. To use: spray or brush canvas. But remember, these are water-soluble materials and treatment should be redone after each exposure to rain.

NOTES

Name of Formula: _____

Date Made: _____

Ingredients and amounts: _____

_____

_____

_____

Label: Ingredients and caution warnings

Observations: _____

_____

_____

_____

_____

- - - - - - - - - -

Name of Formula: _____

Date Made: _____

Ingredients and amounts: _____

_____

_____

_____

Label: Ingredients and caution warnings

Observations: _____

_____

_____

_____

_____

NOTES

Name of Formula: _____

Date Made: _____

Ingredients and amounts: _____

_____

_____

_____

Label: Ingredients and caution warnings

Observations: _____

_____

_____

_____

_____

- - - - - - - - - -

Name of Formula. _____

Date Made: _____

Ingredients and amounts: _____

_____

_____

_____

Label: Ingredients and caution warnings

Observations: _____

_____

_____ _____

_____

_____

For Sports and Camping

Fishline Dressing

It is generally believed that man learned to fish before history was recorded, with the sole object of obtaining food. Sport fishing appears to have been started in England as early as 1496. The first outdoor book to be published, called *The Compleat Angler,* was written by Isaak Walton and made available in the seventeenth century.

There are a number of different ways to sport fish depending on the preference of the fisherman. These would include still fishing, bait casting, trolling, spin casting, spearing, and wet or dry fly fishing. While all of these methods have their place, many sportsmen are adamant in their belief that dry fly fishing is the "king of the sport." Of course, many an argument has centered around this contention.

Dry fly fishing requires that the line, rather than the bait, be cast. This carries the fly, which is attached to the line via a transparent leader, to the spot the fisherman selects. But a dry fly must float to simulate an insect on the surface of the water, so the line must float as well to prevent it from pulling the fly under. To insure against this happening, the line (linen or flax — not monofilament) must be dressed periodically. Here's a formula that makes a good line dressing, simply and inexpensively.

You'll need 2 tablespoons of anhydrous lanolin, 2 tablespoons of petrolatum, and 1 teaspoon castor oil. Put these three ingredients in the top of a double boiler (never over direct heat) and heat until they are melted and can be stirred together. Allow to cool down to just above the solidification point and pour into a mold, such as a small cardboard box. To use, rub line over dressing making sure that all areas are coated.

Golf Ball Distance Improver

Golf, also called "goff," "gauff," and "gawff" in some foreign countries, is a game of frustration, at least for a duffer like me. I've been there. Maybe you have too.

While the Scots claim origin (I may get hit over the head with a bagpipe for this) some believe that its origin was actually in Holland. At any rate it is known that as far back as 1618 golf balls were imported to Scotland from Holland. So I think it's only fair that both of these beautiful countries share the blame for: families that sacrifice father on weekends — broken marriages — the nineteenth hole — clubs wrapped around trees and so forth.

Friction is a deterrent to any object passing through air. For instance, a high performance airplane is assembled with flush rivets on external surfaces to reduce drag and permit the craft to fly faster and farther for the same amount of energy input. The same principle applies to a golf ball. Here's how to take advantage of it.

You'll need silicone oil or silicone oil emulsion from a hardware store and a soft flannel cloth. Measure out 1 cup water, and add 2 tablespoons silicone. If you use the silicone oil, you'll need to mix in 1/4 teaspoon liquid detergent *before* you put the oil in water. Stir water and detergent steadily while adding the oil *slowly*. Lay cloth in a shallow pan and pour mixture over it. Wring excess solution out of cloth and dry in oven. To use, rub over ball frequently.

Mosquito Repellent

Mosquitoes are an enemy of man, and a deadly one at that. Diseases such as yellow fever, malaria, dengue and even the deadly elephantiasis of the tropics, can be attributed to them.

I believe it was Kipling who said "the female is deadlier than the male." And perhaps he was right, at least in the case of the mosquito. The female attacks humans and animals, while the male is content to subsist on the juices of plants.

The best way to kill mosquitoes is to destroy their breeding areas. When you think about their reproductive

For Sports and Camping

capacity — a single female may produce up to five hundred eggs — the productive capacity is enormous. But when you're in your yard on a hot summer night, perhaps enjoying a cookout, and these pests bother you, here's a tried and proven formula that will help.

The ingredients you will need are 2 tablespoons eucalyptus oil, 4 tablespoons talc, and 1 3/4 cups cornstarch. Mix the talc and cornstarch together and then add the eucalyptus oil until it is thoroughly absorbed. To use: Dust on clothes and skin to act as a repellent. Store in glass, metal, or impervious plastic container.

Shotgun and Rifle Cleaning and Polishing Cloth

The true sportsman (and I hope I can be classed as one) regards his fine shotguns and rifles as more than just weapons. Their finely blued metals, precision manufactured, and grained wood stocks and forearms make them things of beauty and should be cared for as such.

Many a winter's evening, long after the hunting season has closed and the ducks and geese are preening their feathers "South of the Border" in sunny Mexico, has found me in front of a fire next to the gun rack with Old Pete, our Chesapeake retriever, asleep next to my chair. This is the time when handling a fine old well-cared-for gun brings back memories of those days in the marsh.

When the hunting season is upon you, there's an easy economical way to protect the external surfaces of your guns against moisture and rust-producing finger marks. You'll need some silicone oil or silicone oil emulsion from a hardware store, and a soft flannel cloth from the rag bag. Measure out 1 cup of water and add 2 tablespoons of the silicone oil emulsion to it. Place the flannel cloth in a shallow pan and pour silicone/water mixture over it. Allow the cloth to soak for 5 to 10 minutes, and wring out excess liquid. Save excess liquid in jar or bottle and retreat cloth occasionally as needed.

When cloth is thoroughly dry, rub *slowly* over all external surfaces of gun, and watch the beautiful sheen come up as the silicone film is deposited. Take the polishing cloth with you in your gun case, and apply to gun after each day in the field.

Note: Most hardware stores carry silicone oil in spray cans; however, some do not carry the water emulsion type. But it's easy to make your own. Simply add a pinch of soap to the water. Add silicone oil with rapid stirring, and the emulsion will form. (To measure from a spray can, hold spray can to edge of spoon, spray gently into spoon allowing silicone to separate from propellant.)

Waterproofing Matches

If you've ever stepped into a hole in your favorite trout stream and gone in over your waders, or become temporarily lost in a woods when it's raining or snowing as I have, you'll agree that a fire can be your best friend. Few things provide more comfort when you're cold and wet. But what a dismal lost feeling it is to find your matches soaked so they won't light. Of course you can buy a waterproof match box, but that isn't really necessary. Matches can be easily waterproofed for pennies. Here's how to do it.

You'll need some large kitchen type matches (we used to call them "lucifers") and about 1/2 cup paraffin wax. Melt the wax in the top of a double boiler (never over direct heat) and adjust heat to just a little above the solidification point. Now dip the individual matches into the molten wax, head down, to about 1/2 the length. Pull out and allow the wax to solidify. If a thicker coat is desired, repeat the process. Put a few of these in likely places such as your tackle box, fishing vest or hunting coat. I hope you never get "dunked" but if you do, you'll be glad you have them.

NOTES

Name of Formula: _____

Date Made: _____

Ingredients and amounts: _____

_____

_____

_____

Label: Ingredients and caution warnings

Observations: _____

_____

_____

_____

_____

- - - - - - - - - -

Name of Formula: _____

Date Made: _____

Ingredients and amounts: _____

_____

_____

_____

Label: Ingredients and caution warnings

Observations: _____

_____

_____

_____

_____

NOTES

Name of Formula: _____

Date Made: _____

Ingredients and amounts: _____
_____
_____
_____

Label: Ingredients and caution warnings

Observations: _____
_____
_____
_____
_____

- - - - - - - - - -

Name of Formula: _____

Date Made: _____

Ingredients and amounts: _____
_____
_____
_____

Label: Ingredients and caution warnings

Observations: _____
_____
_____
_____
_____

6

Animal Care

Animal Care

Animal Bath Powder

We wouldn't think of starting our day without a bath or shower. But admittedly, our dogs and cats are not quite as fastidious so when the time is "ripe" it's necessary to round up old Fido or Tabby and dunk them so they will be acceptable as family members again.

The first thing to do is to catch them. Don't think for a minute that you're fooling them. They know what you plan to do and will disappear. But if you persevere, you will finally "get them in the tub."

And when you do succeed, you should be ready with a good bath powder that will again make them "socially acceptable." Here's the way to make it.

You'll need 1 1/4 cups powdered soap, 1/2 cup tri-sodium phosphate (TSP), 2 tablespoons bicarbonate of soda, and 1 tablespoon boric acid. Dry mix all of these ingredients together thoroughly. To use, put about 3 tablespoons of the mixture in each gallon of warm water. Bathe animal against the grain of the coat and rinse thoroughly. Store in glass, metal, or impervious plastic container. (Caution: TSP is a skin irritant. Use rubber gloves in the preparation of the formula.)

Animal Dandruff Treatment

As in humans, dandruff in animals such as dogs is a condition of the skin whereby small flakes of dead tissue abound. It's believed that the cause is an excessive amount of secretion from the sebaceous glands that are beneath the skin. This condition is further complicated by greater numbers of bacteria and fungi that accompany it.

Among the symptoms of a dandruff condition are skin irritation and itching. So when Fido or Tabby sit down and scratch it should not be assumed that fleas or ticks are necessarily the culprits. Examine the skin carefully by separating the hairs. If you see a dry, flaky surface with small white scales, the following formula frequently helps. But if the condition is severe or persists, have your veterinarian look at it. Our veterinarian tells me that it's not uncommon to find cysts developing in the sebaceous glands, which, of course, require professional attention.

You'll need 1/2 tablespoon salicylic acid, 1 1/2 tablespoons glycerin, and 1 pint of isopropyl alcohol. Mix together. To use, work into coat against the grain of hair. Store in glass or impervious plastic container. (Caution: Isopropyl alcohol is toxic by ingestion and flammable.)

Animal Deodorant Spray

Malodorous dogs are not very pleasant to have around. Unlike cats, who are inherently clean, dogs (at least some that I have had) seem to go out of their way to get themselves messed up by rolling on dead things and other unsavory substances. Whew!

Another rich experience is to be afield with Old Bullet, who hasn't enough sense to stay away from skunks. And then on the ride home in a closed car with the heater on. Again, Whew! I learned long ago to carry a can of tomato juice with me, which is a pretty good skunk smell neutralizer when rubbed into the dog's coat. But for just the "run of the mill" doggy odors — here's a formula that works well.

All you'll need is 1 teaspoon of cedarwood oil, a few drops of liquid detergent, and 1 quart water. We know of course the oil will not mix with the water so we need to disperse it. The detergent will do the trick. Simply mix the detergent into the water, and add the oil, drop by drop with rapid stirring. Store in glass or impervious plastic spray bottle. Use as needed.

NOTES

Name of Formula: _____

Date Made: _____

Ingredients and amounts: _____

_____

_____

_____

Label: Ingredients and caution warnings

Observations: _____

_____

_____

_____

_____

- - - - - - - - - -

Name of Formula: _____

Date Made: _____

Ingredients and amounts: _____

_____

_____

_____

Label: Ingredients and caution warnings

Observations: _____

_____

_____

_____

_____

NOTES

Name of Formula: _____
Date Made: _____
Ingredients and amounts: _____

_____
_____
_____

Label: Ingredients and caution warnings
Observations: _____

_____
_____
_____
_____
_____

- - - - - - - - - -

Name of Formula: _____
Date Made: _____
Ingredients and amounts: _____

_____
_____
_____

Label: Ingredients and caution warnings
Observations: _____

_____
_____
_____
_____

Animal Care

Animal Earache Oil

The ear of an animal, as with humans, is responsible for hearing and balance. There are three parts of the ear which receive these stimuli: external, middle, and inner. When any one of these areas of the ear becomes infected or has foreign bodies interfering with the process the animal will become restless.

There are times when you will see your animal, especially dogs, rubbing his ear along the ground. The animal may back away or growl when you try to pet around the ear. These are all symptoms of ear infection or earache.

When you notice any tenderness or inflammation around the ear, prepare the following formula to relieve the soreness or ache. If the disorder does not appear to go away after application contact your veterinarian for further assistance.

You'll need 3 tablespoons of glycerin and 3 tablespoons almond oil. Mix these ingredients and transfer to glass or plastic dropper bottle. To use, put several drops in affected ear twice each day until condition abates.

Animal Eczema Treatment

Eczema is a skin problem that occurs in both humans and animals. It can affect large areas or be limited to a localized section. It evidences itself by a dry flaking of the skin, with itching and pain. So don't assume that when Fido or Tabby scratches it must be a flea or tick.

If this were to happen to you or me we'd head for the dermatologist, but our animals can't do that. So, because our animals are dependent on us, it's our obligation to watch for signs of eczema and do what we can to make them comfortable. If your animal has symptoms that may indicate the possibility of this condition, here's a formula that could alleviate them. But if the symptoms persist, you'll want to consult your veterinarian, of course.

The Formula Book 2

You'll need 3 tablespoons of tincture of iodine and 3/4 cup glycerin. Mix these two ingredients together and apply to affected areas with cotton. Store in glass or impervious plastic container. (Caution: Iodine is a poison. Handle with care.)

Animal Eyewash

To say that eyesight is invaluable is a gross understatement, of course. As humans we do everything possible to protect ours and we should do the same for our animals that depend on us to such a great extent.

Animals, especially dogs, are in greater danger of experiencing eye irritations than we humans are. The most important difference is that they are closer to dust and dirt, the source of much eye irritation.

Originally, dogs were wild animals and many instincts of that time remain to this day. Have you ever noticed how a dog will turn around a number of times before dropping to the floor or in his bed? This instinct dates back to wild dogs who made a bed that way in tall grass. And other instincts remain as well. Dogs that descended from hunting breeds zip around with their noses close to the ground, while the herding instinct is evident in breeds such as the Collies, Shelties, etc., who put their eyes in jeopardy by their proximity to dirt, dust, pollen, weed seeds, etc.

So whether you take to the field with your hunting dog, or your animals are just pets around the house, take care of their eyes. Here's an inexpensive easy to make formula that can help.

You'll need 1/2 teaspoon boric acid and 1 pint distilled water. Simply mix the boric acid and transfer to an eye dropper bottle. Note: It's wise to sterilize both the bottle and mixing utensil.

NOTES

Name of Formula: _____

Date Made: _____

Ingredients and amounts: _____

_____

_____

_____

Label: Ingredients and caution warnings

Observations: _____

_____

_____

_____

_____

- - - - - - - - - -

Name of Formula: _____

Date Made: _____

Ingredients and amounts: _____

_____

_____

_____

Label: Ingredients and caution warnings

Observations: _____

_____

_____

_____

_____

NOTES

Name of Formula: _____

Date Made: _____

Ingredients and amounts: _____

_____

_____

_____

Label: Ingredients and caution warnings

Observations: _____

_____

_____

_____

_____

- - - - - - - - - -

Name of Formula: _____

Date Made: _____

Ingredients and amounts: _____

_____

_____

_____

Label: Ingredients and caution warnings

Observations: _____

_____

_____

_____

_____

Animal Care

Cat Litterbox Deodorant

Cats are one of the cleanest of all house pets. Housebreaking them is no problem. All they need is an area where they can "relieve themselves," such as a litterbox. Of course, this needs to be kept clean and deodorized.

If a kitten comes into your home, the first thing to do is to provide a "feline comfort station." This can easily be done with a box filled with wood chips. But to prevent odors, an absorbent is needed. And here's a way to do that.

You'll need 3 pounds of wood shavings, and 1/2 pound of bicarbonate of soda. Mix these two ingredients and put in litterbox. Store in glass, metal, or impervious plastic container.

Dog and Cat Coat Dressing

Hair, whether it be human or animal, grows from follicles in the skin. One strand of human hair grows from each follicle; however, in some animals as many as two or three may emerge, which is why they have a denser coat. The inner cells of the hair contain a pigment which accounts for the fact that some dogs or cats are brown, black, white, or a combination of colors.

The general health of humans and animals can frequently be determined by the condition of the hair. Oil glands supply moisture to the strands, which can be excessive and result in an unattractive appearance. Frequent shampooing is essential to remove excess oil that has collected dust and dirt. But some additional oil should then be replaced to dress the coat and provide a neat appearance. Here's a formula for dog and cat coat dressing that we use on our animals, with good results.

You'll need 1 1/2 cups white mineral oil and 1/2 cup pine oil. Mix these ingredients together and apply to coat, working in well. Store in glass, metal, or impervious plastic container.

The Formula Book 2

Flea Spray

We all want our dogs and cats to look nice and neat. But fleas do everything they can to prevent this. These tiny, almost invisible, objects cause our pets to scratch and bite in a vain effort to get rid of them.

Coats of animals can be soiled and roughened by fleas. We must remember: at whatever the cost, our canine and feline friends can't take their furs to the cleaners. This is where the thoughtful, kind, and understanding owner comes in. With spray bottle in hand we attack and never stop to think about whether we are getting rid of the fleas for good. For all we know our homes are the refuge centers for the fleas that escaped.

Take the following formula and spray around the house as well as on the animal. This way you will have no worry of being tossed out of your home by fleas. Here's the formula.

You'll need 2 1/2 cups kerosene, 1/4 cup oleic acid, and 2 tablespoons triethanolamine. Any oil soluble scent may be added if desired. Transfer to plastic spray bottle. To use, spray into animal coat against the direction of the hair. Store in a brown bottle to prevent discoloration and the possible buildup of a rancid odor. (Caution: Kerosene is toxic by ingestion and inhalation and flammable.)

Mange Treatment

Mange, also known as scabies or mites, has been around a very long time. During biblical times the word scabbed was referred to during the period of Moses. Leviticus 22:22. In this piece of scripture we can see the term being applied to the sheep. Domestic animals such as dogs and cats are far from being immune to this problem.

The skin disease is highly contagious and can be transmitted from animal to animal very rapidly. If there is any type of close contact the disease may be trans-

Animal Care

ferred. Because of irritation the animal will become restless and scratch and nibble at the areas that are infested. This irritation is caused by both male and female mites. The male mite remains on the surface of the skin while the female burrows a tunnel up to an inch deep in the skin, where she lays twenty to forty eggs and dies. This process causes the animal to scratch and spread the eggs causing an even larger area to be infected. I know from personal experience in raising, training, and working hunting dogs that few things are more embarrassing than to have the dog stop in the middle of a field trial retrieve, sit down and scratch. The judge would immediately disqualify the entry. And, he'd be perfectly right in doing so. If you have a mild mange problem (serious cases should be seen by a veterinarian) here's a formula that will help.

You'll need 1 cup glycerin, 2 tablespoons cresol, and 2 tablespoons carbolic acid. Mix the cresol and carbolic acid into the glycerin and store in glass or impervious plastic bottle. To use, rub into infected area against the direction of the hair, allow to dry, then rinse thoroughly. (Caution: Carbolic acid (phenol) is very toxic by ingestion, inhalation, and skin absorption. Use rubber gloves when handling and don't breathe vapors.)

NOTES

Name of Formula: _____

Date Made: _____

Ingredients and amounts: _____

_____

_____

_____

Label: Ingredients and caution warnings

Observations: _____

_____

_____

_____

_____

- - - - - - - - - -

Name of Formula: _____

Date Made: _____

Ingredients and amounts: _____

_____

_____

_____

Label: Ingredients and caution warnings

Observations: _____

_____

_____

_____

_____

NOTES

Name of Formula: _____

Date Made: _____

Ingredients and amounts: _____

_____

_____

_____

Label: Ingredients and caution warnings

Observations: _____

_____

_____

_____

_____

- - - - - - - - - -

Name of Formula: _____

Date Made: _____

Ingredients and amounts: _____

_____

_____

_____

Label: Ingredients and caution warnings

Observations: _____

_____

_____

_____

_____

7

Safety and First Aid

Safety and First Aid

Nearly everyone follows basic safety rules every day, probably without even thinking about it. In the kitchen you exercise care when handling boiling liquids and hot things on the stove or in the oven. While driving a car you follow traffic regulations and rules of the road, which are all designed to keep traffic safe. And if you reflect for a moment, you know when it is that you have accidents. It's when you are in a hurry or distracted so that you fail to take the proper care in what you are doing or to notice the things that are going on around you. The times you grab a pot lid and burn your hand, or fail to check in the rear view mirror and back your car into a post, are times when you are trying to do too many things at once or when your mind is focused too intently on something other than what you are doing. This fact is the basis of all safety rules, wherever they occur, in kitchen, traffic, boating, swimming, in shop or garage or laboratory. The more potentially dangerous a situation is, the more elaborate the rules become. In the kitchen they are very general and rarely spelled out. In handling power tools they are more explicit. In handling weapons, safety rules are quite rigorous; and in handling atomic weapons they are explicit, precise, and absolutely inflexible.

These rules, of whatever degree, call our attention to the fact that in that situation we need to take care. If we store this general idea away in our heads, then, even in our more distracted moments, when we are in such a situation, a small signal will go off in our brain saying, "Now you are in a potentially dangerous situation, so to reduce the possibility of accident you had better pay attention."

Those are the general notions of safety. In addition, we would remind you of three specific safety instructions. First, read all labels carefully. Some are purely advertising, but some carry information required by law which is important for you to know and act upon. Second, to the best of your ability, keep dangerous materials out of the reach of children, and let them handle them only under close supervision. From our own experience we know, as we are sure you will too, that even teenagers can get flustered when doing something new for the first time; just recall your state of mind when you learned to drive an automobile. Third, be sure to have labels on all your preparations listing the ingredients, so if a small child or a pet does manage to get into something you will know what it contains.

With respect to first aid, we cannot urge too strongly that, if at all possible, you take the free courses offered by the National Red Cross. We all hope never to have an automobile accident, but we pay good money for insurance every year anyway. A Red Cross first-aid course is like free insurance. You hope never to use the knowledge, but if you do need it sometime, it is valuable. If it is impossible for you to take such a course, you can obtain a good first-aid handbook by writing to your local chapter of the Red Cross. They also offer a free Cardio-Pulmonary-Resuscitation course, or CPR course, which teaches the latest techniques of artificial respiration and closed-chest heart massage. Both of these are excellent, and, in our estimation, essential for everyone. The Red Cross also conducts free swimming classes in many areas of the country; that's another bit of free insurance you can give yourself, not to mention the gain in fun, health, and self-confidence that's in it. If you feel self-conscious about learning to swim at an advanced age, we have two words of advice for you. Overcome it. We have seen classes of youngsters two and three years old, classes of adults from forty to sixty or more years old as well as classes for those in between, and all have enjoyed and profited from the experience. No doubt most of them feel a little self-conscious at first, but when something is beneficial in so many ways, and could save your life, embarrassment should not stop you.

In virtually all major cities, and in thousands of not so major cities and towns, there are poison control centers that have telephones manned twenty-four hours a day. You should have that telephone number in a convenient and obvious place alongside those of the police, fire department, and doctor. They have files on the contents of all poisonous commercial products such as furniture polish, insecticides, and rat poisons, and can tell you the appropriate antidote to give immediately, and whether to induce vomiting or not.

Generally, vomiting should *not* be induced if the person has taken gasoline, kerosene, turpentine, strong acids or alkalis, or if

Safety and First Aid

he is unconscious. These substances cause more damage on the way up than they do in the stomach. If the victim can get down two large glasses of water or milk to help dilute the stuff, this will help. In most other cases, give the person two large glasses of water or milk and then induce vomiting. It is best to remove the poison in this way first, if you know what it is, and if the person is conscious. If he is not conscious he should be placed lying on his stomach with the head turned to one side. If he is conscious have him lie on his back, keep him warm, and then call your doctor or the poison control center. Do not leave the person alone, and be prepared to start mouth-to-mouth resuscitation at the first sign of difficulty in breathing. Recovery can come after hours of artificial respiration, so do not give up. If you are alone and need to call for help, you can stop just long enough to dial the phone. It may be a little tricky holding the phone and giving mouth-to-mouth resuscitation at the same time, but it can be done.

A handy substance to have around the house, and that you can make rather easily, is a universal antidote powder. It consists of 2 parts activated charcoal, 1 part magnesium oxide, and 1 part tannic acid. You can make it in an emergency using burnt toast for the charcoal, milk of magnesia, and instant tea powder for the magnesium and the tannic acid. Give two tablespoons of this in half a glass of warm water. Much of the above information was obtained from *The Merck Manual of Diagnosis and Therapy* and used here with their kind permission.

We would like to repeat, if you are interested in safety and first aid, by far the best thing to do is to take the free Red Cross courses given in most cities and towns. They are usually offered at convenient times in the evening, they are interesting, and they have enabled many people to save lives.

One final and important reminder on safety. When you make a chemical product, *always* label the container, not only as to what the product is, but also the ingredients. In this way, should a child inadvertently consume some of it, your doctor will know what to prescribe as an antidote.

The Formula Book 2

READ THIS — IT COULD SAVE A LIFE

Carbon Tetrachloride

The sale of carbon tetrachloride is banned for home use by the Food and Drug Administration. But somehow it appears that some is still in use. For example, I was doing a question and answer radio program in Kansas City awhile ago, and one person called in to tell me what excellent results she had using it for removing spots. How it gets into homes I don't know. Perhaps some family member works in a lab or industry and brings it home, or it could be a leftover supply. At any rate, *Get rid of it immediately.* It can be lethal, which is why it's banned.

Carbon tetrachloride is dangerous in that it is highly toxic by ingestion, inhalation, and skin absorption and can cause liver damage and other serious complications But even more serious than that is the fact that under certain conditions it can cause immediate death, especially to young children.

When carbon tetrachloride comes in contact with heat it produces phosgene gas, the deadly poison gas of World War I. This gas is over five times the weight of air, and herein lies a great danger. There are many cases on record where carbon tet has been used for removing spots and then a hot iron was used to dry the area. In doing so, phosgene gas was produced, which then fell to the floor where children were playing, causing death.

So if you have any carbon tetrachloride in your home (you may find it in labeled bottles or in those glass globe-type fire extinguishers that hang on the wall), get rid of it. You could easily save a life.

Safety and First Aid

YOU COULD SAVE A LIFE BY READING THIS

Chlorine/Ammonia

As a reader of The Formula Book you know that its primary purpose is to supply formulas and instructions that make it possible for the "do-it-yourselfer" to include chemical products in the list of projects. This individual piece deviates from the basic concept, because I've been reading of a dangerous situation regarding chemicals that you should be made aware of.

Whether you make them yourself or buy the finished product at a store, chlorine bleach and ammonia mixed together produce a gas that is highly irritating to the eyes and lungs, and which, in an enclosed area, can cause death. Likewise, if vinegar (acetic acid) and some lavatory bowl cleaners are mixed, deadly chlorine gas can be formed by the reaction. The seriousness of this is that the products involved are cleaning aids and as such are likely to be stored in the same area in the home, increasing the possibility of an inadvertent mixture — with disastrous results.

If and when formulas for products that could be hazardous when mixed together are given in this book, adequate warnings will be again specifically given. Manufacturers of these cleaning aids, in most cases, do put warnings on their labels. However, in my judgment, they are frequently incomplete and often less conspicuous than they should be.

For the safety of yourself and those around you, it is suggested that you clip this page and tape it in a prominent place where cleaning supplies are kept — which is out of the reach of children, of course. You might want to make copies for several areas of your home.

APPENDIX A

The Four Categories of Formulas Found in *The Formula Book 2*

1. Dry materials that are simply mixed together. Example:
   Fire Extinguishing Powder
   Mix fine silica mason sand and sodium bicarbonate. These are both simply mixed together.

2. Dry or semisolid materials that become liquids when combined with a solvent such as water or alcohol Example:
   Cuticle Remover
   Stir trisodium phosphate (TSP) into glycerin mixing thoroughly, and add water to form a paste. In this type of product we have put a powder into a solution in a solvent, and our end product becomes a liquid.

3. Materials that require heat to turn them from a solid or semisolid into a liquid and back into a solid on cooling. Example:
   Waterproofing Matches
   Melt paraffin wax in double boiler just above solidification point. Dip individual matches into the molten wax to about half the length. Pull out and allow the wax to solidify. In this type of compound we have converted a solid and semisolid into a liquid by melting it, and returned it to a semisolid by cooling.

Appendix A

4. Emulsions. Example:

   Astringent Skin Cream

   Mix mineral oil and beeswax together until the beeswax is melted and mixed with the mineral oil. In separate pan, heat water and stir in borax and powdered alum until dissolved. Pour this mixture slowly into mineral oil and beeswax. When cool, just above the solidification point, add oil-soluble perfume. As we all know, water and oil will not mix unless the oil is combined with an emulsifying agent.

APPENDIX B

Conversion Equivalents

3 teaspoons	equals	1 tablespoon
2 tablespoons	equals	1 liquid ounce
4 tablespoons	equals	1/4 cup
16 tablespoons	equals	1 cup
2 cups	equals	1 pint
2 pints	equals	1 quart
4 quarts	equals	1 gallon
16 ounces	equals	1 pound

METRIC CONVERSIONS

We are approaching the time when the metric system will phase out our conventional system of weights and measures. But this is a confusing transition to make, so many people are wisely beginning to learn it now. To aid in their effort, the following tables are included, and the proportions listed in each formula are expressed in both systems. Thus, by association, learning the equivalents is far easier. For simplification of measurement the metric has been rounded out to 1 decimal and specific gravity average.

CONVERSION FORMULAS

Gallons into Pounds—Multiply 8.33 (wt. 1 gallon of water) by the specific gravity (sg) and the result by the number of gallons. (See any chemical dictionary for the sg of a particular chemical.)

Pounds into Gallons—Multiply 8.33 by the sg and divide the number of pounds by the result.

Appendix B

Milliliters into Grams—Multiply the number of milliliters by the sg.

Grams into Milliliters—Divide the number of grams by the sg.

Milliliters into Pounds—Multiply the number of milliliters by the sg, and divide the product by 453.56 (no. of g. per lb.).

Pounds into Milliliters—Multiply the number of pounds by 453.56 and divide the product by the sg.

Milliliters into Ounces—Multiply the number of milliliters by the sg, and divide the product by 28.35 (no. g. per oz.).

Ounces into Milliliters—Multiply the number of ounces by 28.35 and divide the product by the sg.

CONVERSION FACTORS

Liquid

From	To	Multiply By
Ounces	Milliliters	29.56
Pints	Liters	0.47
Quarts	Liters	0.95
Gallons	Liters	3.78
Milliliters	Ounces	0.03
Liters	Pints	2.10
Liters	Quarts	1.05
Liters	Gallons	0.26

Dry

From	To	Multiply By
Ounces	Grams	28.35
Pounds	Kilograms	0.45
Grams	Ounces	0.035
Kilograms	Pounds	2.21

Conversion Equivalents

FLUID MEASURE

Metric	U.S. Regular
1 milliliter	0.034 ounce
1 liter	33.81 ounces
1 liter	2.10 pints
1 liter	1.05 quarts
1 liter	0.26 gallons

DRY MEASURE

Metric	U.S. Regular
1 gram	0.035 ounce
1 kilogram	35.27 ounces
1 kilogram	2.21 pounds

DRY MEASURE

U.S. Regular	Metric Equivalent
1/8 teaspoon	0.54 grams
1/4 "	1.09 "
1/2 teaspoon	2.19 grams
3/4 "	3.28 "
1 "	4.38 "
1/8 tablespoon	1.77 grams
1/4 "	3.54 "
1/2 "	7.09 "
3/4 "	10.63 "
1 "	14.18 "
1/8 ounce	3.59 grams
1/4 "	7.39 "
1/2 "	14.18 "
3/4 "	21.34 "
1 "	28.35 "

Appendix B

U.S. Regular	Metric Equivalent
1/8 pound	56.69 grams
1/4 "	113.39 "
1/2 "	226.78 "
3/4 "	340.17 "
1 "	453.56 "
1/8 cup	28.34 grams
1/4 "	56.69 "
1/2 "	113.39 "
3/4 "	170.08 "
1 "	226.78 "

LIQUID MEASURE

U.S. Regular	Metric Equivalent
1/8 teaspoon	0.61 milliliters
1/4 "	1.23 "
1/2 "	2.47 "
3/4 "	3.70 "
1 "	4.94 "
1/8 tablespoon	1.84 milliliters
1/4 "	3.69 "
1/2 "	7.39 "
3/4 "	11.08 "
1 "	14.78 "
1/8 ounce	3.69 milliliters
1/4 "	7.39 "
1/2 "	14.78 "
3/4 "	22.17 "
1 "	29.57 "

Conversion Equivalents

U.S. Regular	Metric Equivalent
1/8 cup	29.57 milliliters
1/4 "	59.14 "
1/2 "	118.28 "
3/4 "	177.42 "
1 "	236.56 "
1 pint	473.00 milliliters
1 quart	946.00 "
1/2 gallon	1.89 liters
3/4 "	2.83 "
1 "	3.78 "

APPENDIX C

Temperature Conversion Tables

NOTE: -- The numbers in bold face type refer to the temperature either in degrees Centigrade or Fahrenheit which is to be converted into the other scale. If converting from Fahrenheit to Centigrade the equivalent temperature will be found in the left column. When converting from degrees Centigrade to Fahrenheit, the answer will be found in the column on the right. Interpolation factors are at the bottom right hand corner of the table.

C.		F.	C.		F.	C.		F.	C.		F.	C.		F.	C.		F.
-17.8	0	32	16.0	50	122.0	38	100	212	316	600	1112	593	1100	2012	871	1600	2912
-17.2	1	33.8	10.6	51	123.8	43	110	230	321	610	1130	599	1110	2030	877	1610	2930
-16.7	2	35.6	11.1	52	125.6	49	120	248	327	620	1148	604	1120	2048	882	1620	2948
-16.1	3	37.4	11.7	53	127.4	54	130	266	332	630	1166	610	1130	2066	888	1630	2966
-15.6	4	39.2	12.2	54	129.2	60	140	284	338	640	1184	616	1140	2084	893	1640	2984
-15.0	5	41.0	12.8	55	131.0	66	150	302	343	650	1202	621	1150	2102	899	1650	3002
-14.4	6	42.8	13.3	56	132.8	71	160	320	349	660	1220	627	1160	2120	904	1660	3020
-13.9	7	44.6	13.9	57	134.6	77	170	338	354	670	1238	632	1170	2138	910	1670	3038
-13.3	8	46.4	14.4	58	136.4	82	180	356	360	680	1256	638	1180	2156	916	1680	3056
-12.8	9	48.2	15.0	59	138.2	88	190	374	366	690	1274	643	1190	2174	921	1690	3074
-12.2	10	50.0	15.6	60	140.0	93	200	392	371	700	1292	649	1200	2192	927	1700	3092
-11.7	11	51.8	16.1	61	141.8	99	210	410	377	710	1310	654	1210	2210	932	1710	3110
-11.1	12	53.6	16.7	62	143.6	104	220	428	382	720	1328	660	1220	2228	938	1720	3128
-10.6	13	55.4	17.2	63	145.4	110	230	446	388	730	1346	666	1230	2246	943	1730	3146
-10.0	14	57.2	17.8	64	147.2	116	240	464	393	740	1364	671	1240	2264	949	1740	3164
-9.44	15	59.0	18.3	65	149.0	121	250	482	399	750	1382	677	1250	2282	954	1750	3182
-8.89	16	60.8	18.9	66	150.8	127	260	500	404	760	1400	682	1260	2300	960	1760	3200
-8.33	17	62.6	19.4	67	152.6	132	270	518	410	770	1418	688	1270	2318	966	1770	3218
-7.78	18	64.4	20.0	68	154.4	138	280	536	416	780	1436	693	1280	2336	971	1780	3236
-7.22	19	66.2	20.6	69	156.2	143	290	554	421	790	1454	699	1290	2354	977	1790	3254
-6.67	20	68.0	21.1	70	158.0	149	300	572	427	800	1472	704	1300	2372	982	1800	3272
-6.11	21	69.8	21.7	71	159.8	154	310	590	432	810	1490	710	1310	2390	988	1810	3290
-5.56	22	71.6	22.2	72	161.6	160	320	608	438	820	1508	716	1320	2408	993	1820	3308
-5.00	23	73.4	22.8	73	163.4	166	330	626	443	830	1526	721	1330	2426	999	1830	3326
-4.44	24	75.2	23.3	74	165.2	171	340	644	449	840	1544	727	1340	2444	1004	1840	3344
-3.89	25	77.0	23.9	75	167.0	177	350	662	454	850	1562	732	1350	2462	1010	1850	3362
-3.33	26	78.8	24.4	76	168.8	182	360	680	460	860	1580	738	1360	2480	1016	1860	3380
-2.78	27	80.6	25.0	77	170.6	188	370	698	466	870	1598	743	1370	2498	1021	1870	3398
-2.22	28	82.4	25.6	78	172.4	193	380	716	471	880	1616	749	1380	2516	1027	1880	3416
-1.67	29	84.2	26.1	79	174.2	199	390	734	477	890	1634	754	1390	2534	1032	1890	3434
1.11	30	86.0	26.7	80	176.0	204	400	752	482	900	1652	760	1400	2552	1038	1900	3452
0.56	31	87.8	27.2	81	177.8	210	410	770	488	910	1670	766	1410	2570	1043	1910	3470
0	32	89.6	27.8	82	179.6	216	420	788	493	920	1688	771	1420	2588	1049	1920	3488
0.56	33	91.4	28.3	83	181.4	221	430	806	499	930	1706	777	1430	2606	1054	1930	3506
1.11	34	93.2	28.9	84	183.2	227	440	824	504	940	1724	782	1440	2624	1060	1940	3524
1.67	35	95.0	29.4	85	185.0	232	450	842	510	950	1742	788	1450	2642	1066	1950	3542
2.22	36	96.8	30.0	86	186.8	238	460	860	516	960	1760	793	1460	2660	1071	1960	3560
2.78	37	98.6	30.6	87	188.6	243	470	878	521	970	1778	799	1470	2678	1077	1970	3578
3.33	38	100.4	31.1	88	190.4	249	480	896	527	980	1796	804	1480	2696	1082	1980	3596
3.89	39	102.2	31.7	89	192.2	254	490	914	532	990	1814	810	1490	2714	1088	1990	3614
4.44	40	104.0	32.2	90	194.0	260	500	932	538	1000	1832	816	1500	2732	1093	2000	3632
5.00	41	105.8	32.8	91	195.8	266	510	950	543	1010	1850	821	1510	2750	1099	2010	3650
5.56	42	107.6	33.3	92	197.6	271	520	968	549	1020	1868	827	1520	2768	1104	2020	3668
6.11	43	109.4	33.9	93	199.4	277	530	986	554	1030	1886	832	1530	2786	1110	2030	3686
6.67	44	111.2	34.4	94	201.2	282	540	1004	560	1040	1904	838	1540	2804	1116	2040	3704
7.22	45	113.0	35.0	95	203.0	288	550	1022	566	1050	1922	843	1550	2822	1121	2050	3722
7.78	46	114.8	35.6	96	204.8	293	560	1040	571	1060	1940	849	1560	2840	1127	2060	3740
8.33	47	116.6	36.1	97	206.6	299	570	1058	577	1070	1958	854	1570	2858	1132	2070	3758
8.89	48	118.4	36.7	98	208.4	304	580	1076	582	1080	1976	860	1580	2876	1138	2080	3776
9.44	49	120.2	37.2	99	210.2	310	590	1094	588	1090	1994	866	1590	2894	1143	2090	3794

C.		F.	C.		F.
1149	2100	3812	1427	2600	4712
1154	2110	3830	1432	2610	4730
1160	2120	3848	1438	2620	4748
1166	2130	3866	1443	2630	4766
1171	2140	3884	1449	2640	4784
1177	2150	3902	1454	2650	4802
1182	2160	3920	1460	2660	4820
1188	2170	3938	1466	2670	4838
1193	2180	3956	1471	2680	4856
1199	2190	3974	1477	2690	4874
1204	2200	3992	1482	2700	4892
1210	2210	4010	1488	2710	4910
1216	2220	4028	1493	2720	4928
1221	2230	4046	1499	2730	4946
1227	2240	4064	1504	2740	4964
1232	2250	4082	1510	2750	4982
1238	2260	4100	1516	2760	5000
1243	2270	4118	1521	2770	5018
1249	2280	4136	1527	2780	5036
1254	2290	4154	1532	2790	5054
1260	2300	4172	1538	2800	5072
1266	2310	4190	1543	2810	5090
1271	2320	4208	1549	2820	5108
1277	2330	4226	1554	2830	5126
1282	2340	4244	1560	2840	5144
1288	2350	4262	1566	2850	5162
1293	2360	4280	1571	2860	5180
1299	2370	4298	1577	2870	5198
1304	2380	4316	1582	2880	5216
1310	2390	4334	1588	2890	5234
1316	2400	4352	1593	2900	5252
1321	2410	4370	1599	2910	5270
1327	2420	4388	1604	2920	5288
1332	2430	4406	1610	2930	5306
1338	2440	4424	1616	2940	5324
1343	2450	4442	1621	2950	5342
1349	2460	4460	1627	2960	5360
1354	2470	4478	1632	2970	5378
1360	2480	4496	1638	2980	5396
1366	2490	4514	1643	2990	5414
1371	2500	4532	1649	3000	5432
1377	2510	4550			
1382	2520	4568			
1388	2530	4586			
1393	2540	4604			
1399	2550	4622			
1404	2560	4640			
1410	2570	4658			
1416	2580	4676			
1421	2590	4694			

INTERPOLATION FACTORS

C.		F.
0.56	1	1.8
1.11	2	3.6
1.67	3	5.4
2.22	4	7.2
2.78	5	9.0
3.33	6	10.8
3.89	7	12.6
4.44	8	14.4
5.00	9	16.2
5.56	10	18.0

APPENDIX D

Definitions of Chemicals Used in *The Formula Book 2*

ALMOND OIL: White to yellowish oil, distilled from ground kernels of bitter almonds imported from Spain, Portugal or France. CAUTION: Vapors are toxic.

ALUMINUM POTASSIUM SULFATE DODECAHYDRATE: White crystals or powder, soluble in water. Made by treating kaolin with sulfuric acid.

ALUMINUM STEARATE: White powder, soluble in petroleum and turpentine oil. Made by reacting aluminum salts with stearic acid.

AMMONIUM CHLORIDE (sal ammoniac): White crystals, soluble in water and glycerol. Derived from the reaction of ammonium sulfate and sodium chloride solutions.

AMMONIUM PHOSPHATE DIBASIC: White crystals moderately soluble in water. Derived from the interaction of phosphoric acid and ammonia.

AMMONIUM SULFATE: Gray to white crystals, soluble in water. Made by neutralizing synthetic ammonia with sulfuric acid.

ANHYDROUS LANOLIN (wool fat): Brown jelly, miscible with water. Soluble in benzene, ether, acetone and slightly soluble in cold alcohol.

BICARBONATE OF SODA: See Sodium Bicarbonate.

Appendix D

BORAX (sodium borate): White powder, soluble in water. Mined in the western United States.

BORIC ACID (boracic acid): Colorless odorless white powder, soluble in water, alcohol and glycerin. Made by the addition of hydrochloric or sulfuric acid to a borax solution, and then crystallizing.

CALCIUM CARBONATE (chalk): White powder, slightly soluble in water, highly soluble in acids. Derived principally from limestone.

CALCIUM CHLORIDE: White flakes that decompose in water. Absorptive agent. Calcium chloride and dry-mixed formulas containing it should be stored in airtight containers.

CALCIUM SULFATE: White, odorless crystals or powder, insoluble in water. Occurs in nature as a hydrated form of gypsum, and also as an anhydrite.

CARBOLIC ACID (phenol): Soluble in water and alcohol. Made by the oxidation of cumene. CAUTION: toxic by ingestion, inhalation and skin absorption.

CARNAUBA WAX (brazil wax): Yellow to brown hard lumps, melting point 84°-86°C. Collected from the leaves of the Brazilian wax palm, *Copernicia cerifera*.

CASTOR OIL (ricinus oil): Pale yellow oil, soluble in alcohol. Derived from pressing the seeds of the castor bean, *Ricinus communis*.

CEDARWOOD OIL: Is an odorless essential oil extracted from cedar bark and wood, soluble in alcohol.

CHALK: See Calcium Carbonate.

CLAY (hydrated aluminum silicate): Tan powder, ranging in particle size from 150 to less than 1 micron. Ab-

Definitions of Chemicals

sorbs water to form a plastic mass. Derived from nature by natural weathering, crushing, and screening of rock.

COPPER SULFATE (blue vitriol, bluestone): Blue crystals, lumps, or powder. Soluble in water or methanol. Made by the action of dilute sulfuric acid on copper or its oxides. CAUTION: Highly toxic by ingestion.

CORN OIL (maize oil): Pale yellow liquid, partially soluble in alcohol. The germ is removed from the kernel and cold pressed.

CORNSTARCH: White amorphous powder, derived from corn or maize.

CRESOL (cresylic acid): Colorless or yellowish to pinkish crystals with a characteristic odor. Soluble in alcohol, glycol and dilute alkalies. Slightly soluble in water. CAUTION: toxic and irritant.

DEODORIZED KEROSENE: Kerosene that has been treated chemically to mask its odor. CAUTION: toxic if taken internally. Flammable.

DEXTRIN: A yellow or white powder that's water soluble. Made by heating dry starch or by treating starch with a dilute acid.

DIATOMACEOUS EARTH (kieselguhr, diatomite): A bulky light material containing 88% silica. The balance is made up of the skeletons of small prehistoric plants related to algae. Can be had in either brick or powdered form.

ETHYL ALCOHOL (vodka): See Appendix E.

ETHYLENE GLYCOL MONOETHYL ETHER (cellosolve): Colorless liquid, miscible with water and hydrocarbons. Flash point 120°F. Flammable and toxic by ingestion.

Appendix D

EUCALYPTUS OIL (cineol eucalyptol or cajeputal): A colorless oil having a camphorlike odor and pungent, cooling, spicy taste. Miscible with alcohol, ether and glacial acetic acid. Made by distillation of eucalyptus leaves. Slightly toxic if taken internally.

FORMALDEHYDE: An aqueous solution. Made by oxidation of synthetic methanol. CAUTION: highly toxic by ingestion, inhalation or skin contact.

FUEL OIL (furnace oil): Number 1 or 2 grade. Oil used in home heating furnaces. CAUTION: Flammable.

FULLER'S EARTH: A porous colloidal aluminum silicate of 1 micron or less, having high adsorptive power. Mined in Florida, England, and Canada.

GELATIN: White to yellow powder, soluble in hot water. Made by boiling animal by-products with water. Will absorb up to ten times its weight of water.

GLYCERIN (glycerol): A clear, colorless syrupy liquid, soluble in water and alcohol. Made by the hydrogenation of carbohydrates with a nickel catalyst.

HOUSEHOLD AMMONIA: A dilute solution of ammonium hydroxide (usually about 5% in water). CAUTION: fumes may be irritating to eyes and nasal passages. Never combine household ammonia with chlorine bleach. Dangerous gasses will result. Do not breathe vapors, avoid contact with skin.

HYDRATED LIME (calcium hydroxide): White powder, soluble in glycerin. Made by the action of water on calcium oxide. CAUTION: Skin irritant.

HYDROGEN PEROXIDE: Colorless dilute aqueous solution. May be further diluted with water. CAUTION: Highly toxic in concentrated form. Relatively low toxicity in dilute aqueous solution.

Definitions of Chemicals

ISOPROPYL ALCOHOL (isopropanol): White sweet smelling liquid. Soluble in water, ether, or alcohol. Made by treating propylene with sulfuric acid and then hydrolyzing. CAUTION: mildly toxic by inhalation and ingestion. Flammable.

KEROSENE: Oily liquid distilled from petroleum. CAUTION: Toxic if taken internally. Flammable.

LANOLIN (wool fat): Yellow to light gray semisolid, soluble in ether or chloroform. Extracted from raw wool and refined.

LAURYL PYRIDINIUM CHLORIDE: Mottled tan semisolid, soluble in water. May be mildly irritating to skin.

LINSEED OIL: Amber to brown oil, soluble in alcohol. Made by refining raw linseed oil. Warning: Dries when exposed to air. Keep in airtight container.

LIGHT LUBRICATING OIL: Amber to red liquids of varying viscosity, refined from crude petroleum oil.

MAGNESIUM SULFATE (epsom salts): Colorless crystals, soluble in water and glycerol. Made by the action of sulfuric acid on magnesium oxide.

MINERAL OIL—WHITE (liquid petrolatum): Colorless transparent oil, distilled from petroleum. Flammable.

MONOCALCIUM PHOSPHATE: See Superphosphate.

NEAT'S-FOOT OIL: A pale yellow oil, soluble in alcohol and kerosene. Made by boiling, in water, the shinbones and feet, without hoofs, of cattle. The oil and fat are then separated.

OLEIC ACID (red oil): Yellow to red oily liquid, soluble in alcohol and organic solvents. Derived from animal tallow or vegetable oils.

Appendix D

OLIVE OIL: Pale yellow to greenish liquid, nondrying. Only slightly soluble in alcohol. Soluble in ether, chloroform or carbon disulfide. Oil is cold-pressed from the olive fruit and then refined.

PARADICHLOROBENZENE (moth crystals): White volatile crystals, soluble in alcohol, benzene and ether. Made by chlorination of monochlorobenzene. Moderately toxic by ingestion. Irritant to eyes.

PARAFFIN OIL: An oil that is pressed from paraffin distillate. For characteristics, see paraffin wax. Flammable.

PARAFFIN WAX: White waxy blocks, soluble in benzene, warm alcohol, turpentine, and olive oil. Made by distilling crude petroleum oil. Flammable.

PEANUT OIL (groundnut oil): Yellow oil, soluble in petroleum ether, carbon disulfide and chloroform. Can be saponified by alkali hydroxides to form a soap.

PETROLATUM (mineral wax, petroleum jelly, mineral jelly): Colorless to amber oil translucent mass, soluble in benzene, ether, chloroform and oil. Melting point, 60°C. Made by the distillation of still residues from steam distillation of paraffin based petroleum. Flammable.

PINE OIL: Colorless to amber oily liquid. Miscible with alcohol. Made by the steam distillation of pine wood.

PORTLAND CEMENT: White to gray powder composed of lime, alumina, silica and iron oxide.

POTASSIUM NITRATE (niter, saltpeter): Transparent or white crystals or powder, soluble in water. CAUTION: Dangerous fire and explosion risk when subjected to shock or heating. Oxidizing agent. Handle carefully.

Definitions of Chemicals

PUMICE POWDER: A gently abrasive fine powder milled from porous rock found in nature.

PYRETHRIN EXTRACT: A powder obtained from milling ground pyrethrum flowers. Usually mixed with kerosene or other solvents such as petroleum. CAUTION: moderately toxic if taken internally.

RAPE SEED OIL (colza oil, rape oil): Pale yellow viscous liquid, soluble in ether, chloroform and carbon disulfide. Made by expression or solvent extraction of rape seeds.

ROSIN: Translucent amber chips, soluble in alcohol, ether, glacial acetic acid and oil. Derived by steam distillation of the sap of pine trees.

SALICYLIC ACID (ortho-hydroxy benzoic acid): White powder, soluble in alcohol, oil of turpentine and ether. Made by treating a hot solution of sodium phenolate with carbon dioxide.

SASSAFRAS LEAVES: The leaves of the plant *Sassafras albidum*.

SAWDUST: Residual material resulting from sawing/sanding wood.

SHELLAC (garmet lac, gum lac, stick lac): A natural resin secreted by the insect Laccifer and deposited on the trees in India. Soluble in alcohol.

SILICA GEL: Hard, white lumps, crystals or powder. Regenerative adsorbent, having a vast internal porosity in relation to its outside surface. Made by the reaction of sulfuric acid and sodium silicate.

SILICA MASON SAND: A fine sand used in mortars. Mined from natural deposits.

Appendix D

SILICONE OIL: An oily liquid, soluble in other oils. Made by treating silicon chemically.

SILICONE OIL EMULSION: A milky slippery liquid that can be further diluted with water to any desired concentration. Made by the mixture of silicone oil, emulsifier and water.

SODA ASH (sodium carbonate): Grayish-white powder, soluble in water. Mined in areas such as Great Salt Lake, or can be made by the Solvay ammonia soda process.

SODIUM BICARBONATE (baking soda): White powder, soluble in water. Made by treating a saturated solution of soda ash with carbon dioxide.

SODIUM BORATE: An odorless, light crystal or powder soluble in water; effervesces when in contact with water, releasing oxygen.

SODIUM CHLORIDE (salt): White crystals soluble in water and glycerol. Made by the evaporation of salt brine.

SODIUM METAPHOSPHATE: White powder, soluble in water.

SODIUM METASILICATE: A crystalline silicate. White granules, soluble in water.

SODIUM PERBORATE: White odorless powder or crystals. Decomposes in water to release oxygen. Made by electrolysis of a solution of borax and soda ash. Moderately toxic by ingestion.

SODIUM PHOSPHATE DIBASIC: White powder, soluble in water and alcohol. Made by precipitating calcium carbonate from a solution of dicalcium phosphate with soda ash.

Definitions of Chemicals

SODIUM SILICATE (waterglass): Clear viscous liquid, soluble in water. Made by the fusion of sand and soda ash. May be irritating and caustic to skin and mucous membranes.

SODIUM SULFATE (salt cake): White crystals or powder, soluble in water. A byproduct of hydrochloric acid production from salt and sulfuric acid.

SODIUM THIOSULFATE: White crystals or powder, soluble in water and oil of turpentine. Made by heating a solution of sodium sulfite with powdered sulfur.

STEARIC ACID: Waxlike solid, soluble in alcohol ether, chloroform or carbon disulfide. Made by hydrogenation of oleic acid.

SUPERPHOSPHATE (acid phosphate): Water-soluble powder, made by the action of sulfuric acid on insoluble rock.

TALC (talcum, mineral graphite, steatite): A mined mineral (magnesium silicate), white-gray pearly color with a greasy feel.

TALLOW: Solid fatty material found in beef.

TARTARIC ACID: White crystalline powder, soluble in water and alcohol. Made from maleic anhydride and hydrogen peroxide.

TINCTURE OF BENZOIN: Clear to pale yellow liquid having a slight camphor odor. The crystals from which the tincture is made, are derived from the condensation of benzaldehyde in a cyanide solution.

TRIETHANOLAMINE (TEA, TRI): Colorless viscous hygroscopic liquid, miscible with water and alcohol, a soap base. Made by the reaction of ethylene oxide and ammonia. May be somewhat irritating to skin and mucous membranes.

Appendix D

TRISODIUM PHOSPHATE (TSP) (sodium phosphate dibasic): Colorless crystals or white powder, soluble in water and alcohol. Made by precipitating calcium carbonate from a solution of dicalcium phosphate with soda ash. Skin irritant, use rubber gloves. Moderately toxic by ingestion.

TURPENTINE: Colorless, clear, oil liquid. Made by steam distillation of turpentine gum. CAUTION: toxic if taken internally. Flammable. Handle with care.

UREA (carbamide): White crystals or powder, soluble in water, alcohol, and benzene.

VERMICULITE: Crystalline-type structure with high porosity. Insoluble, except in hot acids. Used as a filler in concrete, and for thermal insulation.

VINEGAR (dilute acetic acid): Brown liquid dilutable with water. Made by fermentation of fruit and grains. May be distilled to remove brown color, after which it is known as white vinegar.

WHITE BEESWAX: Wax from the honeycomb of frames in the beehive. White color is obtained by bleaching the natural yellow wax. Soluble in chloroform, ether, and oils. Melting point $62°$-$65°C$.

ZINC CHLORIDE: White crystals or crystalline powder, soluble in water, alcohol, and glycerin. Made by the action of hydrochloric acid on zinc. CAUTION: Toxic.

ZINC OXIDE (chinese white, zinc white): Coarse white to gray powder, soluble in acids and alkalies. Made by oxidation of vaporized pure zinc. CAUTION: Poisonous if taken internally.

APPENDIX E

A Treatise on Denatured Alcohols

ETHYL ALCOHOL/DENATURED ETHYL ALCOHOL

Alcohols are widely used in many areas of chemistry, and especially in compounding of formulas such as those found in *The Formula Book 2*. As a matter of fact, it would be hard to conceive of being able to make many of the compounds without it. But, based on the mail we have received from many teachers and students, there seems to be some confusion over the two primary types, i.e., ethyl alcohol in its pure form, and ethyl alcohol that has been denatured, denatured alcohol. We hope this section will promote a better understanding for those who may not be completely clear on the subject.

Ethyl alcohol (ethanol, grain alcohol) (C_2H_2OH or CH_3CH_2OH), is a clear colorless liquid having a melting point of -117°C., and a boiling point of 78.5°C. It is miscible in any proportion with water or ether, and is soluble in a sodium hydroxide (caustic soda) solution. Flammable, it burns in air with a bluish transparent flame, producing water and carbon dioxide as it burns. Density is 0.789 at 20°C.

Absolute (anhydrous) ethyl alcohol is obtained by the removal of water. One process for accomplishing this is to react the water in the alcohol, with calcium oxide and then distill the alcohol.

Ethyl alcohol is made by (A) the fermentation of grains and fruits, and also directly from dextrose, (B) by absorption of ethylene from coal or petroleum gas,

Appendix E

and then water reaction, and (C) by the reduction of acetaldehyde in the presence of a catalyst.

Ethyl alcohol is used in tremendous quantities in beverages which are taxed by the federal government. There are many other uses as well, such as in pharmaceuticals, tinctures, and extracts for internal use, where it is not taxed as it is for beverages. For these uses however, a special tax-free permit must be obtained from the Alcohol and Tobacco Unit of the Federal government. Permits of this type are available to educational institutions as well. However, for small quantity use, just buying a bottle of 95 or 100 proof vodka is much less complicated.

Denatured alcohol is ethyl alcohol (the same as is used in beverages), except that it has been adulterated with other chemicals that make it unfit for beverage use, while still retaining its other characteristics. Therefore, denatured alcohol is not taxed as pure ethyl alcohol is, making it very much less expensive.

There are two basic types of denatured alcohol, Completely Denatured (CDA), and Specially Denatured (SDA). The denaturants that are used are specified by the Alcohol and Tobacco Tax Unit, and depend on the end use of the alcohol. For example, a denaturant acceptable for use in alcohol to be used as an industrial solvent would be entirely unacceptable for use in a body lotion or mouthwash because of its degree of toxicity and irritating properties. Therefore, the type of denatured alcohol must be chosen for the compound it's to be used in. Following is a list of general compound classifications and the code number of the denatured alcohol approved for each. You will notice that a given type of denaturant may be used in the alcohol that is used in many different formulas. From the following chart it will be seen that Specially Denatured Alcohol, Type 40, is approved for use in a number of applications such as: bath preparations, bay rum, cleaning solutions, colognes, etc. Therefore, in purchasing denatured alcohol it is practical to select the type that fits as many uses as possible. While the approved types of denatured alcohol for specific uses is mandatory for a manufacturer who resells, it

A Treatise on Denatured Alcohols

does not apply to the individual making the product for his own use. However, in the interest of safety, it is *highly recommended* that only approved types for the specific formulas be used.

DENATURED ALCOHOL USE	ALCOHOL and TOBACCO TAX APPROVED TYPE
Animal Feed Supplements	35A.
Antifreeze	1.
Antiseptic Bathing Solutions	46.
Antiseptic Solutions	23A, 37, 38B, 38F.
Bath Preparations	1, 3A, 3B, 23A, 30, 36, 38B, 39B, 39C, 40, 40A, 40B, 40C.
Bay Rum	23A, 37, 38B, 39, 39B, 39D, 40, 40A, 40B, 40C.
Brake Fluids	1, 3A.
Candy Glazes	13A, 23A, 35, 35A.
Cellulose Coatings	1, 23A, 30.
Cleaning Solutions	1, 3A, 23A, 23H, 30, 36, 39B, 40, 40A, 40B, 40C.
Coatings	1, 23A.
Colognes	38B, 39, 39A, 39B, 39C, 40, 40A, 40B, 40C.

Appendix E

Cutting Oils	1, 3A.
Dentifrices	31A, 37, 38B, 38C, 38D.
Deodorants (Body)	23A, 38B, 39B, 39C, 40, 40A, 40B, 40C.
Detergents (Home Use)	1, 3A, 23A, 23H, 30, 36, 39B, 40, 40A, 40B, 40C.
Detergents (Industrial)	1, 3A, 23A, 30.
Disinfectants	1, 3A, 3B, 23A, 23H, 27A, 27B, 30, 37, 38B, 39B, 40, 40A, 40B, 40C.
Drugs and Medicinal Chemicals	1, 2B, 2C, 3A, 6B, 12A, 13A, 17, 29, 30, 32.
Duplicating Fluids	1, 3A, 30.
Dye Solutions	1, 3A, 23A, 30, 39C, 40, 40A, 40B, 40C.
Fuel Uses	1, 3A, 28A.
Fungicides	1, 3A, 3B, 23A, 23H, 27A, 27B, 30, 37, 38B, 39B, 40, 40A, 40B, 40C.
Hair and Scalp Preparations	3B, 23A, 23F, 23H, 37, 38B, 39, 39A, 39B, 39C, 39D, 40, 40A, 40B, 40C.
Inks	1, 3A, 13A, 23A, 30, 32, 33
Insecticides	1, 3A, 3B, 23A, 23H, 27A, 27B, 30, 37, 38B, 39B, 40, 40A, 40B, 40C.

A Treatise on Denatured Alcohols

Iodine Solutions and Tinctures	25, 25A.
Lacquer Thinners	1, 23A.
Liniments	27, 27B, 38B.
Lotions and Creams (Body, Face and Hands)	23A, 23H, 31A, 37, 38B, 39, 39B, 39C, 40, 40A, 40B, 40C.
Mouthwashes	37, 38B, 38C, 38D, 38F.
Perfumes and Tinctures	38B, 39, 39B, 39C, 40, 40A, 40B, 40C.
Petroleum Products	1, 2B, 3A.
Plastics-Cellulose	1, 2B, 3A, 12A, 13A, 30.
Plastics and Resins	1, 2B, 3A, 12A, 13A, 30.
Polishes	1, 3A, 30, 40, 40A, 40B, 40C.
Preserving Solutions	1, 3A, 12A, 13A, 22, 23A, 30, 32, 37, 38B, 42, 44.
Resin Coating (Natural)	1, 23A.
Resin Coating (Synthetic)	1, 23A, 30.
Room Deodorants	3A, 22, 37, 38B, 39B, 39C, 40, 40A, 40B, 40C.
Rubbing Alcohol	23H.
Scientific Instruments	1, 3A.

Appendix E

Shampoos	1, 3A, 3B, 23A, 27B, 31A, 36, 38B, 39A, 39B, 40, 40A, 40B, 40C.
Shellac Coatings	1, 23A.
Soaps (Industrial)	1, 3A, 23A, 30.
Soaps (Toilet)	1, 3A, 3B, 23A, 30, 36, 38B, 39B, 39C, 40, 40A, 40B, 40C.
Soldering Flux	1, 3A, 23A, 30.
Solutions (Miscellaneous)	1, 3A, 23A, 30, 39B, 40, 40A, 40B, 40C.
Solvents and Thinners	1, 23A.
Stains (Wood)	1, 3A, 23A, 30.
Sterilizing Solutions	1, 3A, 12A, 13A, 22, 23A, 30, 32, 37, 38B, 42, 44.
Toilet Water	38B, 39, 39A, 39B, 39C, 40, 40A, 40B, 40C.
Unclassified Uses	1, 3A.
Vinegar	18, 29, 35A.

DENATURING FORMULAS

While the formulas for denaturing ethyl alcohol for various applications are not particularly relevant to the user of *The Formula Book* because the alcohol you purchase will already be denatured, they are of general interest in that they show the different degrees of contamination required for uses in different product formulas. For this reason they are included in this section.

A Treatise on Denatured Alcohols

ALCOHOL & TOBACCO TAX,
APPROVED TYPES   DENATURING FORMULAS

1)   100 gallons ethyl alcohol, 5 gallons wood alcohol.

2B)   100 gallons ethyl alcohol, 5 gallons methyl alcohol.

2C)   100 gallons ethyl alcohol, 33 pounds metallic sodium and 1/2 gallon benzene.

3A)   100 gallons ethyl alcohol, 5 gallons methyl alcohol.

3B)   100 gallons ethyl alcohol, 1 gallon pine tar.

6B)   100 gallons ethyl alcohol, 1/2 gallon pyridine bases.

12A) 100 gallons ethyl alcohol, 5 gallons benzene.

13A) 100 gallons ethyl alcohol, 10 gallons ethyl ether.

17)   100 gallons ethyl alcohol, 6 4 fl. oz. bone oil.

18)   100 gallons ethyl alcohol, 100 gallons vinegar (90Gr.)

23A) 100 gallons ethyl alcohol, 10 gallons acetone.

23F) 100 gallons ethyl alcohol, 3 pounds salicylic acid, USP, 1 pound resorcin, USP, 1 gallon bay oil, USP.

23H) 100 gallons ethyl alcohol, 8 gallons acetone, 1.5 gallons methyl isobutyl ketone.

27A) 100 gallons ethyl alcohol, 35 pounds camphor, USP, 1 gallon clove oil, USP.

27B) 100 gallons ethyl alcohol, 1 gallon lavender oil, USP, 100 pounds medicinal soft soap, USP.

28A) 100 gallons ethyl alcohol, 1 gallon gasoline.

Appendix E

29) 100 gallons ethyl alcohol, 1 gallon 100% acetaldehyde.

30) 100 gallons ethyl alcohol, 10 gallons methyl alcohol.

31A) 100 gallons ethyl alcohol, 100 pounds glycerol, USP, 20 pounds hard soap.

32) 100 gallons ethyl alcohol, 5 gallons ethyl ether.

37) 100 gallons ethyl alcohol, 45 fluid ounces eucalyptol USP, 30 ounces by weight thymol, 20 ounces by weight menthol USP.

38B) 100 gallons ethyl alcohol, 10 pounds menthol, USP.

38C) 100 gallons ethyl alcohol, 10 pounds menthol, USP, 1.25 gallons formaldehyde, USP.

38F) 100 gallons ethyl alcohol, 6 pounds boric acid, USP, 1-1/3 pounds thymol, 1-1/3 pounds chlorothymol, and 1-1/3 pounds menthol, USP.

39) 100 gallons ethyl alcohol, 9 pounds sodium salicylate USP, 1.25 gallons extract of quassia, 1/8 gallon tert.-butyl alcohol.

39A) 100 gallons ethyl alcohol, 60 ounces quinine, 1/8 gallon tert.-butyl alcohol.

39B) 100 gallons ethyl alcohol, 2-1/2 gallons diethyl phthalate, 1/8 gallon tert.-butyl alcohol.

39C) 100 gallons ethyl alcohol, 1 gallon diethyl phthalate.

39D) 100 gallons ethyl alcohol, 1 gallon bay oil, 50 ounces by weight quinine sulphate.

40) 100 gallons ethyl alcohol, 1-1/2 ounces brucine, 1/8 gallon tert.-butyl alcohol.

A Treatise on Denatured Alcohols

40A) 100 gallons ethyl alcohol, 1 pound sucrose octaacetate, 1/8 gallon tert.-butyl alcohol.

40B) 100 gallons ethyl alcohol, 1/16 ounce denatonium benzonate, 1/8 gallon tert.-butyl alcohol.

40C) 100 gallons ethyl alcohol, 3 gallons tert.-butyl alcohol.

42) 100 gallons ethyl alcohol, 80 grams potassium iodine, USP, 109 grams red mecuric iodide.

44) 100 gallons ethyl alcohol, 10 gallons n-butyl alcohol.

APPENDIX F

Selection of Materials

The selection of materials depends on the end use of the product. For example, the selection of denatured alcohol for use in a paint or varnish thinner would be entirely different from the choice of a product that would be in contact with the skin. (See Appendix D.)

There are two basic grades of chemicals used: 1) U.S.P., and 2) Manufacturing or Technical.

1. *U.S.P.*, is an abbreviation for the United States Pharmacopoeia which is the official federal book of chemicals and drugs. This publication sets up the standards of purity and other specifications that the manufacturer must comply with. Generally speaking, U.S.P. grades are used in compounds that are taken internally, or come in contact with delicate areas of the body that require pure materials. An example of this is where a material such as magnesium sulfate (epsom salts) is contained in a product for internal use, it must be U.S.P. grade.

2. *Manufacturing or Technical Grade.*
In this category, the standards for purity are understandably less than in the U.S.P. grade, in that the end product does not directly affect human health. For example, if the epsom salts were to be used in a foot bath, the purity requirements would not be the same as for internal use, and the Manufacturing or Technical grade would be acceptable.

Appendix F

There is a substantial difference in the cost of these two grades of materials, therefore, the selection should always be made on the basis of the end use.

The *odor and color,* used in a preparation is largely a matter of personal choice, and usually has no effect on the function of the compound itself. For example, in the formula for Face Lotion, the perfume in the product has no effect on the properties it imparts to the skin. However, if perfume or color is desired, it must be of a type that is compatible with the compound it is to be used in.

Dyes and perfumes fall into three general categories: (1) those that are soluble in oil, (2) those that are soluble in water or alcohol, and (3) those that are suitable for use in an emulsion.

Examples of these types are as follows:

Type One; is soluble in oil and would be used in liquids, semisolids, and solids having an oil base such as Baby Oil.

Type Two; is soluble in water and alcohol and would therefore be used in compounds such as Face Lotion where the base is water and alcohol.

Type Three; is an emulsion type and logically, is used in emulsions. Each formula that requires a perfume or dye has the type specified in the formula itself.

But a word of warning. Perfumes and dyes are in highly concentrated form, and should be used very sparingly.

APPENDIX G

Utensils and Equipment

The formulas found in *The Formula Book 2* are designed for small volumes of the finished product, requiring a minimum of equipment to formulate. The following utensils are required.

1. Several glass measuring cups. (See Figure 2.)
2. A set of mixing bowls made of glass, ceramic or plastic. (See Figure 10.)
3. A wood fork with spacing of about 1/8" between tines. (See Figure 3.)
4. An egg beater. (See Figure 4.) An electric mixer, with beaters and bowl, is helpful but not essential. If it has variable speeds, it can be used for both wet and dry mixing, saving a great deal of time and assuring a "good blend."
5. A stem type thermometer is convenient, but again, not absolutely essential. (See Figure 5.) If one is not available, remember that water gives off a mild vapor at 140°F., a moderate vapor at 160°F., a heavy vapor at 180°F. and heavy steam at the boiling point.
6. A supply of wood tongue depressors. (See Figure 8.) These are smooth, cheap and readily available from any druggist. They make excellent mixing sticks, and are inexpensive enough to be disposable, eliminating a lot of "cleaning up."
7. Paper cups are ideal for small batch formulating. They are inexpensive, disposable and can be easily numbered or marked with a felt marker.
8. Double boilers are required in many instances. These should be Pyrex. (See Figure 6.)

Appendix G

9. A rubber syringe for measuring out drops. (See Figure 7.)

10. A set of standard measuring spoons. (See Figure 11a.)

11. A plastic cone and filter paper, such as is used in coffee making. (See Figure 9.) While filtering a liquid compound after it is finished is not usually essential, it is always desirable, in that a clearer, better looking product results.

12. Containers for the finished product are a matter of personal preference. In most homes, jars and bottles are available. If they are to be purchased, many supermarkets carry them, and drugstores have them for their own use. Larger quantities can be had from bottle distributors, listed in the Yellow Pages.

All chemicals that are stored in containers should be labeled, regardless of whether they are a raw material or a finished compound. This is basic, and must be followed in the interest of safety. Keep all chemicals out of the reach of children, and note the contents on the label. In this way if a child, or even an unsuspecting adult, should accidentally consume the contents, the doctor would know what treatment to initiate. While these formulas have been chosen with an eye to safety, many materials normally regarded as safe can be dangerous if taken internally, or to excess. Here's an example of a safe label.

```
┌─────────────────────────────────────────────┐
│  This Bottle Contains  _____ │
│  Its Ingredient(s) are:                      │
│                                              │
│                                              │
│  Keep out of reach of children.              │
│                                              │
│  Made by _____   │
│                                              │
│  Date _____   │
│              KEEP BOTTLE SEALED              │
└─────────────────────────────────────────────┘
```

This Bottle Contains ____________________
Its Ingredient(s) are:

Keep out of reach of children.

Made by ____________________

Date ____________________

KEEP BOTTLE SEALED

This Bottle Contains ____________________
Its Ingredient(s) are:

Keep out of reach of children.

Made by ____________________

Date ____________________

KEEP BOTTLE SEALED

This Bottle Contains ____________________
Its Ingredient(s) are:

Keep out of reach of children.

Made by ____________________

Date ____________________

KEEP BOTTLE SEALED

This Bottle Contains ____________________
Its Ingredient(s) are:

Keep out of reach of children.

Made by ____________________

Date ____________________

KEEP BOTTLE SEALED

This Bottle Contains ____________________
Its Ingredient(s) are:

Keep out of reach of children.

Made by ____________________

Date ____________________

KEEP BOTTLE SEALED

This Bottle Contains ____________________
Its Ingredient(s) are:

Keep out of reach of children.

Made by ____________________

Date ____________________

KEEP BOTTLE SEALED

This Bottle Contains ____________________
Its Ingredient(s) are:

Keep out of reach of children.

Made by ____________________

Date ____________________

KEEP BOTTLE SEALED

This Bottle Contains ____________________
Its Ingredient(s) are:

Keep out of reach of children.

Made by ____________________

Date ____________________

KEEP BOTTLE SEALED

This Bottle Contains ____________________
Its Ingredient(s) are:

Keep out of reach of children

Made by ____________________

Date ____________________

KEEP BOTTLE SEALED

This Bottle Contains ____________________
Its Ingredient(s) are:

Keep out of reach of children.

Made by ____________________

Date ____________________

KEEP BOTTLE SEALED

This Bottle Contains ____________________
Its Ingredient(s) are:

Keep out of reach of children.

Made by ____________________

Date ____________________

KEEP BOTTLE SEALED

This Bottle Contains ____________________
Its Ingredient(s) are:

Keep out of reach of children.

Made by ____________________

Date ____________________

KEEP BOTTLE SEALED

Utensils and Equipment

Illustrations

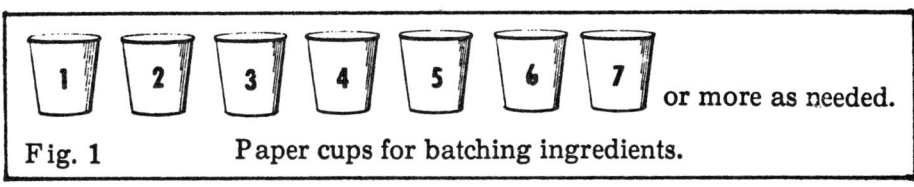
Fig. 1   Paper cups for batching ingredients. (or more as needed.)

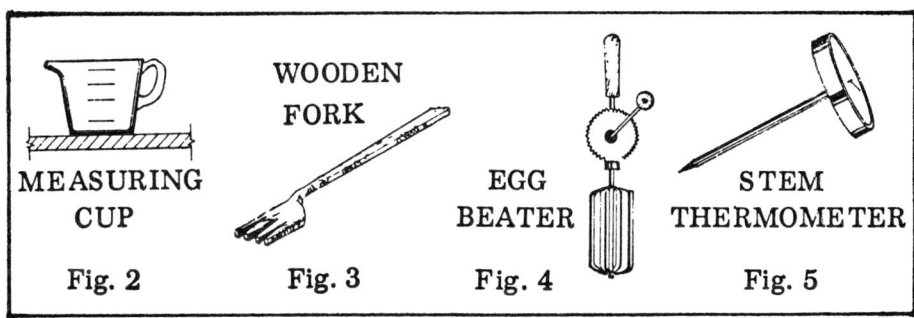

MEASURING CUP — Fig. 2

WOODEN FORK — Fig. 3

EGG BEATER — Fig. 4

STEM THERMOMETER — Fig. 5

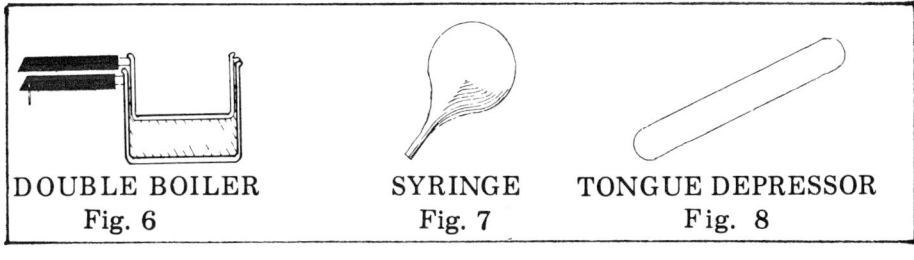

DOUBLE BOILER — Fig. 6

SYRINGE — Fig. 7

TONGUE DEPRESSOR — Fig. 8

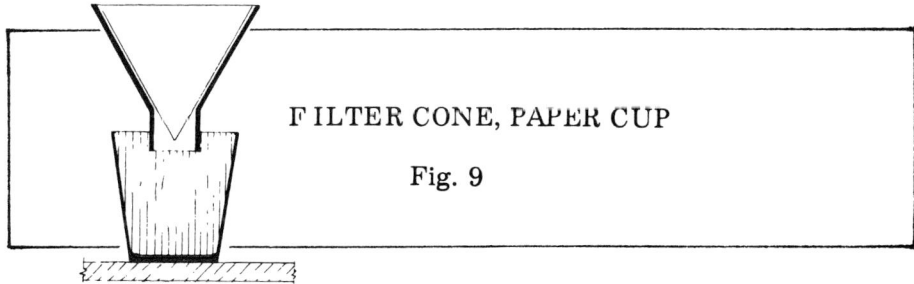

FILTER CONE, PAPER CUP

Fig. 9

Appendix G

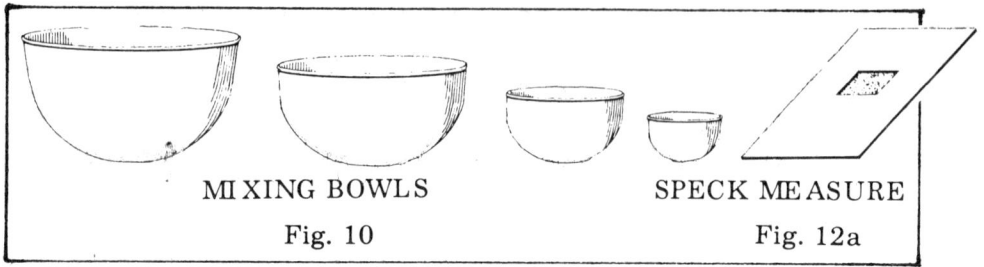

MIXING BOWLS
Fig. 10

SPECK MEASURE
Fig. 12a

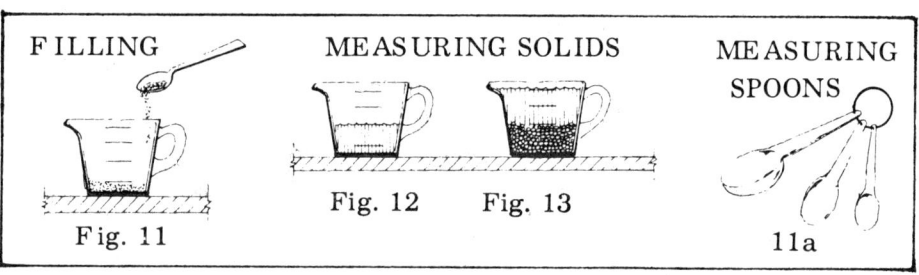

FILLING
Fig. 11

MEASURING SOLIDS
Fig. 12   Fig. 13

MEASURING SPOONS
11a

APPENDIX H

Formulating Procedures

The ingredients in each formula must be combined in the correct sequence, because a chemical reaction may take place and a deviation from that sequence could prevent it. One of the best ways to insure against error is to use separate containers for the ingredients, numbered in the order that they are to be incorporated into the compound. (See Appendix G, Figure 1.) Paper cups work well for this, in that they are inexpensive, disposable, and can be easily numbered with a felt marker.

The correct measurement of ingredients is important Always have the utensil that is being measured into on a level surface. (See Figure 2, Appendix G.) Measure accurately to the line of the quantity specified. Avoid touching container to eliminate the possibility of compacting the material, which would increase its quantity (See Figure 11, Appendix G.)

Use standard measuring spoons, not eating spoons. A spoonful is a measuring spoon that is filled level with the top. Dip spoon in material to rounding, and then scrape excess off with a knife. (Figure 11a, Appendix G.)

A speck is the amount of powdered or granular material that will lie in a 1/4" square marked on a piece of paper. (See Figure 12a, Appendix G.)

When a formula calls for a portion of a cup of lump or semisolid material that is not *water soluble,* use this method. If you want to measure 1/2 cup of lump paraffin for example, pour *cold* water in a measuring cup to the 1/2 cup line. Next, add lumps of paraffin to the water until the water level reaches the 1 cup line. Pour out the

Appendix H

water, and the paraffin in the cup will equal 1/2 cup. (See Figures 12 and 13, Appendix G.)

Follow instructions given in each individual formula, and *always* follow labeling instructions given in Appendix G

APPENDIX I

Sources of Chemicals

Below is a list of ingredients and sources of supply used in The Formula Book 2, followed by the number of times these ingredients are used, for the convenience of the consumer who must buy these ingredients in small quantities.

ALMOND OIL: drugstore or drug distributors, 2
ALUMINUM STEARATE: paint store or chemical supply house, 1
ALUMINUM SULFATE: drugstore, drug distributor or industrial chemical supplier, 3
AMMONIUM CHLORIDE: drugstore, drug distributor or industrial chemical supplier, 1
AMMONIUM PHOSPHATE: drug distributor, chemical supply house or feed and grain store, 1
AMMONIUM SULFATE: drugstore, drug distributor, chemical suppy house, 4
ANHYDROUS LANOLIN: drugstore or chemical supply house, 1

BEESWAX: drugstore or hobby shop, 2
BICARBONATE OF SODA (baking soda): grocery store, 6
BORAX: grocery or hardware store, 7
BORIC ACID: drugstore or chemical supply house, 8

CALCIUM CARBONATE: drugstore, chemical supply house, feed and grain store or building material dealer, 8
CALCIUM CHLORIDE: drugstore or county and state highway departments, 1
CALCIUM SULFATE: chemical supply house or building material dealer, 1

Appendix I

CARBOLIC ACID: drugstore or chemical supply house, 1
CASTOR OIL: drugstore or chemical supply house, 4
CEDARWOOD OIL: drugstore or chemical supply house, 1
CHALK (calcium carbonate): drugstore, chemical supply house, feed and grain store or building material dealer, 8
CLAY (hydrated aluminum silicate): chemical supply house, building material dealer or ceramic shop, 1
COPPER SULFATE: drugstore or chemical supply house, 1
CORN OIL: grocery store, 1
CORNSTARCH: grocery store, 5
CRESOL: drugstore or chemical supply house, 1

DEODORIZED KEROSENE: service station or oil distributor, 1
DIATOMACEOUS EARTH: chemical supply house or building material dealer, 2

ETHYL ALCOHOL (vodka): liquor store, 1
ETHYLENE GLYCOL MONOETHYL ETHER: drugstore, 1
EUCALYPTUS OIL: drugstore, 1

FORMALDEHYDE: drugstore or chemical supply house, 1
FUEL OIL: service station or oil distributor, 2
FULLER'S EARTH (diatomaceous earth): chemical supply house or building material dealer, 2

GELATIN: grocery store, 2
GLYCERIN: drugstore, 16

HOUSEHOLD AMMONIA: grocery store, 1
HYDRATED LIME: drugstore, feed and grain store, chemical supply house, 1
HYDROGEN PEROXIDE: drugstore, chemical supply house, 1

ISOPROPYL ALCOHOL: drugstore or solvent distributor, 16

KEROSENE: paint or hardware store, oil distributor, 2

Sources of Chemicals

LANOLIN: drugstore or chemical supply house, 1
LAURYL PYRIDINIUM CHLORIDE: chemical supply house, 1
LINSEED OIL: hardware or paint store, 1
LIGHT LUBRICATING OIL: service station or oil distributor, 1

MAGNESIUM SULFATE (epsom salts): drugstore or chemical supply house, 1
MINERAL OIL: drugstore or chemical supply house, 6
MONOCALCIUM PHOSPHATE (superphosphate): feed and grain store or chemical supply house, 1

OLEIC ACID: drugstore or chemical supply house, 1
OLIVE OIL: grocery store, 1

PARADICHLOROBENZENE (moth crystals): drugstore or chemical supply house, 1
PARAFFIN WAX: grocery store, 7
PEANUT OIL: grocery store, 1
PETROLATUM: drugstore, oil distributor or chemical supply house, 3
PINE OIL: drugstore or chemical supply house, 3
PORTLAND CEMENT: building material dealer, 1
POTASSIUM NITRATE: drugstore or chemical supply house, 2
POWDERED PUMICE: hardware store, 1
PYRETHRIN: garden supply store, 1

ROSIN: drugstore or chemical supply house, 1

SALICYLIC ACID: drugstore or chemical supply house, 3
SASSAFRAS LEAVES: drugstore or chemical supply house, 1
SHELLAC: hardware store or chemical supply house, 1
SHORTENING: grocery store, 1
SILICA GEL: refrigeration service, 1
SILICA MASON SAND: building material dealer, 2
SILICONE OIL: foundry or foundry supply dealer, 1

Appendix I

SILICONE OIL EMULSION: foundry or foundry supply dealer, 3
SODA ASH: hardware store or swimming pool supplier, 2
SODIUM BICARBONATE (baking soda): grocery store, 6
SODIUM BORATE: drugstore, 1
SODIUM CHLORIDE (salt): grocery store or feed and grain store, 3
SODIUM METASILICATE: drugstore or laundry supply dealer, 1
SODIUM PERBORATE: drugstore or chemical supply house, 5
SODIUM SILICATE (waterglass): drugstore or foundry supply dealer, 1
SODIUM SULFATE: drugstore or chemical supply house, 1
SODIUM THIOSULFATE: photographic supply store, 2
SOY FLOUR: health food store, 1
STEARIC ACID: drugstore or hobby shops, 1
SUPERPHOSPHATE: feed and grain store or chemical supply house, 1

TALC: drugstore, 5
TALLOW: meat market, 1
TARTARIC ACID: drugstore or chemical supply house, 2
TINCTURE OF BENZOIN: drugstore, 1
TRIETHANOLAMINE: drugstore or chemical supply house, 2
TRISODIUM PHOSPHATE (TSP): hardware store or chemical supply house, 7
TURPENTINE: hardware or paint store, 1

UREA: chemical supply house, 1

VERMICULITE: building material dealer, 1
VINEGAR: grocery store, 5

WHEAT FLOUR: grocery store, 2
WHITE BEESWAX: drugstore or hobby shop, 2

ZINC OXIDE: drugstore or ceramic shop, 1

SPECIALIZED SOURCES OF CHEMICALS

Chem-Pack, Inc., P.O. Box 27163, Tucson, Arizona 85726. Chemicals are available in small quantities by mail from this firm. Almost anything that could possibly be needed will be found here. However, it is cheaper to buy the more common chemicals from local sources.

Manufacturers: Many chemical manufacturers have local offices in principal cities. Frequently they are listed under the product you wish to locate. For example, under Silicones in the Yellow Pages may be found Dow Corning, or Union Carbide. All principal manufacturers are listed, under the product you seek, in the O.P.D. Chemical Buyers Directory, Schnell Publishing Company. Most libraries will have a copy.

APPENDIX J

pH Preferences of Some Plants

In light of upward spiraling prices and a world food shortage, growing our own food is becoming a way of life for many of us. And it's fun. But it's work too. Ask any weekend gardener who discovers new muscles on Monday morning. So it just makes sense to take advantage of any practice that will increase yields for the same amount of effort. And one of the most rewarding things that can be easily done is to provide the plant with soil that has been adjusted to the most desirable degree of acidity or alkalinity. This is known as adjusting the pH of the soil.

For practical purposes the range of pH we are concerned with is from 4 to 8, with 7 representing neutral. As you go down the scale from 7, the acidity increases. As you go up the scale from 7, the alkalinity increases. The procedures for testing the pH of soil are simple, and will be covered in another paragraph.

Now let's go through a typical example of adjusting the soil in a given area to make it ideal for the plants we wish to grow there. By reference to the following table, we find that asparagus, beets, cabbage, carrots, cauliflower, celery, lettuce, onions and parsley all have a pH preference range of 7 to 8 with the ideal being 7.5 on the scale, which is slightly alkaline. So naturally it follows that these vegetables should be planted in the same area where the soil has been adjusted to a pH of approximately 7.5. Of course, the same procedure applies to other areas where plants of other pH preferences will be

Appendix J

grown. In the case of house plants, each pot of soil will be individually adjusted to the plant's preference.

To determine and alter soil pH, you will need an inexpensive tester. There are a number of these on the market that may be obtained from garden supply centers and swimming pool supply dealers. The writer's preference is to use chemically treated paper that changes color to indicate pH. This paper comes in rolls about 1/4" wide housed in a plastic tape-type dispenser. The procedure we use is as follows.

Step 1) Let's assume you have set aside an area 5' wide by 20' in length to grow the group of vegetables that prefer a pH of 7.5. Your objective is to adjust the soil in that area to a pH of approximately 7.5. First, get a glass container that will hold at least a pint of water. (A Pyrex measuring cup works fine.) You will also need either a plastic or wooden spoon. Rinse the inside of the glass container and the spoon with *distilled* or *demineralized* water. These are commonly used for steam irons, and are available at any supermarket. *Be sure your hands do not touch the inside of the glass or bowl of the spoon,* as this could contaminate your reading.

Step 2) To obtain an average sample of the area in which you want to determine and adjust the pH, place a spoonful of soil taken from locations in the area about 3' apart, and several inches below the surface. Mix these samples together in the glass, thoroughly. Next, cover the soil with distilled or demineralized water to about 1/2" over the soil. Now, using your spoon, mix the water and soil thoroughly and allow glass container to stand undisturbed. In a short time, the soil will settle to the bottom of the container leaving the clear water over it.

Step 3) You are now ready to determine what the pH of the area is. Pull out about a 2" strip of the chemically treated paper from the dispenser and hold by one end. Do not allow your fingers to come into contact with the rest of the paper strip. Immerse one end of the paper in the clear water over the soil and compare the wet section of the strip with the color chart found on the side of the

pH Preferences of Some Plants

container. The match of color between the strip and chart will tell you the pH of the soil.

Step 4) Formulas for adjusting the pH of house plants are not generally economical for larger areas such as gardens. For this use, the most effective and economical method is as follows.

To alkalize the soil, i.e., to raise the pH number, the least expensive and best material to use is ground limestone. The formula is 6 pounds of limestone for each 100 square feet of area to increase the pH by one point. Therefore, if the pH of your soil is 6.5 and the desired level is 7.0, you would need to work in 3 pounds of limestone for the 100 square foot area.

On the other hand, if the soil needed to be acidified, the formula would be to use either aluminum sulphate or powdered sulphur, whichever is lowest in cost and most readily available in your area. Applied at the rate of 2 pounds for each 100 square feet of area, the pH will be lowered by one point on the scale. Thus, if your soil had a pH of 8 and you wanted 7.5, you would have to work in 1 pound of either material over the 100 square foot area.

We are constantly adjusting soil pH on our research and testing facility near Tucson, Arizona, and find two methods of application to be effective. Either a small seed spreader with an adjustable discharge slot, or a rotary seeder or duster, also adjustable, will do a good job of giving even distribution over the area. After the material has been distributed, we work it into the soil with a rototiller. Of course for small areas, an ordinary garden rake will do just as well.

It is important to remember that some time is required for the full acidifying or alkalizing process to complete itself. Therefore, the most desirable time to test and adjust is in the fall, and then make a final check before planting time.

Appendix J

Following is a list of vegetables, fruits, flowers and grasses, showing their acceptable pH range. The optimum value is at the midpoint of the range. For example, the acceptable range for asparagus is 7-8, so the optimum value is 7.5.

VEGETABLES AND FRUITS

Name	pH Range	pH Optimum
Asparagus	7 — 8	7.5
Beets	7 — 8	7.5
Cabbage	7 — 8	7.5
Carrots	7 — 8	7.5
Cauliflower	7 — 8	7.5
Celery	7 — 8	7.5
Lettuce	7 — 8	7.5
Onions	7 — 8	7.5
Parsley	7 — 8	7.5
Plums	7 — 8	7.5
Broccoli	6 — 7	6.5
Brussels Sprouts	6 — 7	6.5
Corn	6 — 7	6.5
Cucumbers	6 — 7	6.5
Peas	6 — 7	6.5
Peppers	6 — 7	6.5
Radishes	6 — 7	6.5
Raspberries	6 — 7	6.5
Rhubarb	6 — 7	6.5
Spinach	6 — 7	6.5
Melons	6 — 7	6.5
Beans	5 — 6	5.5
Citrus	5 — 6	5.5
Parsnips	5 — 6	5.5
Potatoes	5 — 6	5.5
Grapes	5 — 6	5.5
Squash	5 — 6	5.5
Strawberries	5 — 6	5.5
Tomatoes	5 — 6	5.5
Turnips	5 — 6	5.5

pH Preferences of Some Plants

FLOWERS

Barberry	7 — 8	7.5
Calendula	7 — 8	7.5
Geranium	7 — 8	7.5
Morning Glory	7 — 8	7.5
Nasturtium	7 — 8	7.5
Petunia	7 — 8	7.5
Poppy	7 — 8	7.5
Sweet Pea	7 — 8	7.5
Alyssum	6 — 7	6.5
Aster	6 — 7	6.5
Candytuft	6 — 7	6.5
Cauna	6 — 7	6.5
Carnation	6 — 7	6.5
Chrysanthemum	6 — 7	6.5
Columbine	6 — 7	6.5
Cosmos	6 — 7	6.5
Crocus	6 — 7	6.5
Dahlia	6 — 7	6.5
Dogwood	6 — 7	6.5
Feverfew	6 — 7	6.5
Gladiolus	6 — 7	6.5
Hollyhock	6 — 7	6.5
Hyacinth	6 — 7	6.5
Hydrangia (Pink)	6 — 7	6.5
Iris	6 — 7	6.5
Marigold	6 — 7	6.5
Pansy	6 — 7	6.5
Peony	6 — 7	6.5
Rose	6 — 7	6.5
Snapdragon	6 — 7	6.5
Tulip	6 — 7	6.5
Violet	6 — 7	6.5
Zinnia	6 — 7	6.5
Delphinium	5 — 6	5.5
Easter Lily	5 — 6	5.5
Fern	5 — 6	5.5
Lupine	5 — 6	5.5
Begonia	5 — 6	5.5
Phlox	5 — 6	5.5

Appendix J

Primrose	5 — 6	5.5
Azalea	4 — 5	4.5
Holly	4 — 5	4.5
Hydrangia (Blue)	4 — 5	4.5
Rhododendron	4 — 5	4.5

GRASSES

Blue Grass	7 — 8	7.5
Clover	7 — 8	7.5
Squirrel Tail Grass	7 — 8	7.5
Red Clover	6 — 7	6.5
Bermuda Grass	6 — 7	6.5
Colonial Bent Grass	6 — 7	6.5
Creeping Bent Grass	6 — 7	6.5
Italian Rye Grass	6 — 7	6.5
Perennial Rye Grass	6 — 7	6.5
Rough Blue Grass	6 — 7	6.5
Sudan Grass	5 — 6	5.5
Panic Grass	4 — 5	4.5

Index

Acidifying or alkalizing potted plant soil, 93
Adhesive tape remover, 23
Alcohol resistant treatment for wood, 23
Animal bath powder, 117
Animal dandruff treatment, 117
Animal deodorant spray, 118
Animal earache oil, 121
Animal eczema treatment, 121
Animal eyewash, 122
Ant repellent, 93
Antiseptic cleaner — all purpose, 24
Antiperspirant foot powder, 59
Antistatic spray for rugs, 27
Astringent skin cream, 59
Auto fuel ice preventative, 87
Automobile and boat top dressing, 87
Auto windshield cleaner, 88
Auto windshield insect remover, 88

Baby oil II, 60
Baby powder, 63
Baking pan antistick, 27
Ballpoint ink remover for hands, 63
Barbecue flame extinguisher, 105

Bathtub and sink cleaner, 28
Bay rum, 64
Beauty clay, 64
Blackboard cleaner, 31
Blackhead remover, 65
Boat top dressing, 87
Boot dubbing, 105

Callus softener, 66
Canvas fire retardant, 106
Carbon tetrochloride, 136
Carpet cleaner, 31
Cat litter box deodorant, 125
Caterpillar tree bands, 94
Ceramic tile cleaner, 32
Chemical flower garden, 95
Chlorine/ammonia, 137
Christmas tree fire retardant and needle preservative, 32
Cleaner,
   auto windshield, 88
   bathtub and sink, 28
   carpet, 31
   dry hand, 68
   leather, 76
   liquid porcelain, 42
   paint and wall, 46
   range, 46
   sink disposal, 48
   vinyl, 51
Coffee extract, 33

Index

Compost making, 95
Cuticle remover, 66

Dance floor wax, 34
Dandruff treatment, 67
Deodorant,
    animal spray, 118
    cat litter box, 125
    general purpose, 39
    refrigerator, 47
    underarm pads, 81
Disinfectant for shoes, 68
Dog and cat,
    bath powder, 117
    coat dressing, 125
    dandruff treatment, 117
    deodorant spray, 118
    earache oil, 121
    eczema treatment, 121
    eyewash, 122
    flea spray, 126
    mange treatment, 126
Dry hand cleaner, 68

Earwax softener, 69
Effervescent bath salts, 70
Eyelash and eyebrow conditioner, 71

Face lotion, 72
Face powder, 72
Facial bleach, 73
Facial pore closer, 74
Finger stain remover, 74
Fire extinguishing powder, 37
Fire retardant for canvas, 106
Fire retardant for Christmas trees, 32
Fire retardant paper, 38
Fireplace flame colors, 37
Fireplace soot remover, 38
Fishline dressing, 109
Flea spray, 126
Foot bath, oxygen, 78
Foot powder, 75

Garden, compost making, 95
Garden insecticide — all purpose, 97
Gasoline vapor lock compound, 89
General purpose deodorant and disinfectant, 39
Golf ball distance improver, 109
Grass stain remover, 40

Hand and face lotion, lanolin, 76
Hand cream, protective, 78
Hand cleaner, dry, 68
Hand lotion, winter, 81
Heating or cooling filter cleaning compound, 40
Hydroponic plant food, 98

Ice cube release, 41

Lanolin hand and face lotion, 76
Leather cleaner, 76
Library paste, 41
Liquid porcelain cleaner, 42
Liquid underarm deodorant, 77
Lubricating stick, 42

Mange treatment, 126
Mildewproofing for book bindings, 43
Mosquito repellent, 110
Moth repellent, 44

Oil and grease spot remover, 45
Oxygen foot bath, 78

Paint and wall cleaner, 46
Potted plant fertilizer, 99
Potted plant soil acidifying or alkalizing, 93
Protective hand cream, 78

Rabbit repellent, 100
Range cleaner and polish, 46

Index

Refrigerator deodorant, 47
Repellent,
  ant, 93
  caterpillar, 94
  flea, 126
  mosquito, 110
  moth, 44
  rabbit, 100
Rubbing alcohol compound, 79
Rugs, antistatic spray, 27

Sink disposal cleaner, 48
Shoes and boots,
  boot dubbing, 105
  disinfectant, 68
Shotgun and rifle cleaning
    cloth, 111
Soapless rug cleaner, 48
Stain remover,
  oil and grease, 45
  grass, 40
  tar and nicotine, 79

Tar and nicotine stain
    remover, 79
Toilette water, 80

Underarm deodorant pads, 81

Vinyl cleaner, 51

Wallpaper remover, 51
Waterproofing matches, 112
Water softener — all
    purpose, 52
Wax, dance floor, 34
Winter hand protective
    lotion, 81
Wood, alcohol resistant
    treatment for, 23
Wood floor bleach II, 53

Norman Stark is the author of the best-selling *Formula Book*. His nationally syndicated column is featured in more than 100 major daily newspapers. Stark, who holds over a dozen patents on his inventions, has met with remarkable success in his supplementary textbook *The Formula Manual*, from which this book and *The Formula Book 1* evolved. *The Formula Manual* has been sold to thousands of school libraries and chemistry departments since Stark first began working on it in 1970.

His work in this area has required considerable expansion; he has established his own laboratory in Tucson for analyzing existing products, creating new formulas, and undertaking thorough testing of his formulas.

Stark's work in chemistry goes back to 1940, when he founded the Stark Research Corporation to conduct research, development, and manufacturing in the chemical field.

Shortly after the beginning of World War II, Stark was asked by the military to develop a process for making fuel tablets — small bars of a combination of wax and finely ground wood flour encased in a chemically impregnated carton — to be used to heat field rations. After making millions of fuel tablets, Stark was then put to work developing a high-speed process for making the Sterno-type canned heat. Finally, during the war, Stark was commissioned to develop a continuous high-speed process for making candles, a need created by the fact that troops were moving ahead of generating equipment on the fighting fronts and were in desperate need of light.

After the end of the war, Stark discontinued the manufacturing aspects of his concern and devoted his efforts solely to research and development. Since that time, many of his projects have resulted in patents and licensing agreements with America's leading corporations. Frequently, when Stark licensed a process or a material, he would act as a consultant to the company involved.